Belonging

Adventures
in Church Membership

by Donald N. Bastian

Light and Life Press
Indianapolis, Indiana

Copyright © 1978 by
Light and Life Press
Revised 1980
Revised 1983
Revised 1986
Revised 1990

Seventh printing 1993

Printed in the United States of America
by Light and Life Press, Indianapolis, IN 46214

ISBN 0-89367-044-8

All scripture quotations, unless otherwise indicated, are taken from the HOLY BIBLE, NEW INTERNATIONAL VERSION®. NIV®. Copyright © 1973, 1978, 1984 by International Bible Society. Used by permission of Zondervan Publishing House. All rights reserved. Quotations marked TEV (Today's English Version) are from the Good News Bible: Copyright © American Bible Society 1966, 1971, 1976. Used by permission. Quotations marked NASB, © The Lockman Foundation 1960, 1962, 1968, 1971, 1972, 1973, 1975 are used by permission. Quotations marked *Phillips*, are from *The New Testament in Modern English, Revised Edition,* © J. B. Phillips 1958, 1960, 1972, and are used by permission. Quotations marked JB, are from *The Jerusalem Bible,* copyright © 1966 by Darton, Longman & Todd, Ltd., and Doubleday & Company, Inc. Used by permission of the publisher. Quotations marked KJV are from the King James Version.

Table of Contents

INTRODUCTION

This is a book about belonging.

Everybody needs to belong--from the four-pound preemie in the hospital incubator to the ninety-two-year-old grandma, comatose in the nearby nursing home.

Only the recluse living three miles up the railroad tracks seems to have overcome the need. And even he walks to town every second Saturday to buy a few groceries at the co-op--with money printed by the government.

This is a book about belonging to the church. The church comes in all shapes and sizes and goes under many different names. It is affected by geography, climate, folk ways, language, ethnic characteristics, and local leaders. Always, however, beneath superficial colorations, the church when it is authentic is the people of God.

Like a great cosmic vine, the universal church has many branches. One of those branches bears the name Free Methodist. This is a book about belonging to the Free Methodist Church.

People have problems with belonging these days. They want to and they don't want to. They are drawn and repelled by the same body. Some Christians struggle with such feelings for years.

As a pastor, I conversed for many hours with Christians who didn't understand their own contradictory feelings. They needed help in sorting out ideas that God would approve from ideas that had no place dominating a Christian's life.

I have written now with these problems in mind. I have tried to put them under Christian scrutiny.

Are institutions evil simply because they are institutions? Why do Christians need to talk about their roots and heritage--isn't the Bible enough? Who needs to worry about Christian doctrine if he simply loves the Lord? And what about the innumerable decisions one has to make as a disciple of Jesus Christ?

These are some of the questions I have confronted in this book.

When you have finished studying it, you may or may not agree with its point of view. I have kept that possibility open throughout. But I hope you will keep it open, too, and that you will read with an awareness that I have considered the options.

This book is an invitation and a guide. It is an invitation to belong to a church that is conservative in doctrine, evangelical in spirit, and concerned to be an instrument in God's hand to bring the message of full salvation to the world.

The book is a guide to belonging and pinpoints what membership entails and offers.

Every chapter is incomplete, and I have felt this keenly as I have written. Important matters are only touched on--left to be filled out where you live and perhaps through years of further study.

In a sense it is an international book. Parts of it have been written over the Aleutian Chain, in the Chicago O'Hare Airport, in a bedroom in Saskatchewan, in a hotel room in Manila while waiting for a strayed suitcase to catch up to me, in a Holiday Inn in Florida, and wherever else in my travels I've had time to pull a sheaf of notes from my briefcase and arrange them on my lap.

Much of it has been written or corrected in my downstairs study in Toronto. Some of it is a carry-over from an earlier book, *The Mature Church Member*.

I express thanks for help given. Dr. Lloyd Knox, former publisher, now retired. Dr. Dorsey Brause, former denominational director of Adult Ministries, read the finished chapters and offered helpful suggestions. My son Donald, who edits for a living, looked at some of the chapters and had things to say which I've listened to attentively. The Reverend G. Roger Schoenhals, former editorial director of Light and Life Press, put the finishing touches on the manuscript and saw it through production.

I owe special thanks to my secretary, Mrs. Barbara Sackett, who has gone home more than once with the feeling of typewriter keys tingling at her finger tips. Through all the reams, she did not complain.

My greatest single helper in this project, next to the Lord, has been my wife, Kathleen. She is a good thinker, a good listener, and a good reader; and through all the extra evenings and Saturdays across the past seven months she has been unfailingly patient.

When you read some parts of this book, you may think I have a romantic view of my church. I see the possibility myself but I express it another way: The church has loved me and guided me from my childhood. It has borne with me patiently and has given me countless opportunities to serve the Lord. Love like this begets love, and the more you love, the less you see the blemishes. Or, at least, the less the blemishes show against the whole. If that's what romanticism entails in this case, I'm guilty.

Donald N. Bastian

CHAPTER ONE

The church represents the eternal God. It has its roots in the ancient past, and its creeds make frequent references to the age to come. It is obviously not in tune with the secular humanist mind. The irony is, however, that those who take seriously the larger views of reality, held by the church, experience most richly the here and now. They handle the unresolved contradictions of life better, and their joy is more profound.

The Pros and Cons of Belonging

Ken and Wanda and their twelve-year-old daughter, Janice, stepped forward in a Free Methodist Church one June Sunday morning and offered themselves for membership. They were almost total strangers to the congregation.

Almost, but not quite. A retired missionary couple, Harold and Lucille, lived next door and knew them well. They had visited over the hedge, looked out for one another's property, and watered one another's plants.

Only two months before that special June day, Harold and Lucille had started a home Bible study with them. One night a week, all five sat around the dining room table reading from their workbooks, sharing insights, and asking the kind of fresh questions first-time Bible readers come up with easily.

During those informal nights, Ken and Wanda shared bits and pieces out of their life stories. Wanda had gone to church a little when she was a child but Ken had not. He didn't think highly of the church. Sensing this, Harold and Lucille never invited them to attend. They just kept meeting them around the dining room table and talking across the hedge and loving them and praying for them daily.

I met Ken and Wanda the Sunday before they offered themselves for membership. My wife and I were guests in the home of Harold and Lucille, and I was to preach at their church that Sunday night.

Surprisingly, Ken and Wanda came. It was the first time they had ever seen the inside of a Free Methodist church. After the service, Harold and Lucille invited them to their home. Over fresh strawberries and ice cream, we all conversed easily, Bibles in our laps. The subject: how to become a Christian.

By the time we got to Revelation 3:20, Ken was ready. He opened his heart simply to Jesus Christ, and Wanda followed just as simply. What Ken told us then surprised even his close friend Harold. Ken had been lying awake at night thinking about the Bible. Two months of careful shepherding had brought results. Ken and Wanda were converted one Sunday and, at their eager request, received baptism and joined the church the next.

It was like that in New Testament times. People heard the gospel, believed in Jesus Christ, received baptism, and were "added to the church." The steps followed each other naturally. There was no reason to wait.

It should be that way today, but it isn't always.

Some new and some not-so-new Christians have conflict over belonging to the church.

Recently in Florida, my wife and I were overnight guests in the home of new-found friends, a Michigan couple spending the winter months in the south. During breakfast, I mentioned that I was thinking a great deal these days about the matter of belonging to the church. My hostess smiled.

"We've only been members of the Free Methodist Church seven years," she said, "even though we've been associated with the church all our lives."

"Why did you take so long to join?" I asked.

She was silent for a few moments. Then she said, "I think it was because I wanted to be honest in joining. I wanted to be able to live up to every requirement, and I wasn't ready to join until I could."

I turned to my host. "And what kept you back?"

He smiled and said impishly, "My wife." They both laughed. Old Adam was laying the blame on his Eve again.

But then he became serious. "I think at first it was my wife. I didn't want to join until she did. But you know," he went on slowly, "after you've said no two or three times, it gets to be a bit of a game saying no. It wasn't that we weren't asked. We were asked regularly. And we went to church as faithfully as anyone, and took part."

Objections Some Christians Raised

If you have struggled with the question of belonging, you are not alone. During twenty-one years as a pastor I heard many objections to membership from Christians:

1. I don't want to join this church because I don't know how long I'm going to live in this community. My firm may transfer me at any time.
2. I worship here, I know, but my membership is in

another denomination (or congregation) and I don't want to switch loyalties.

3. I once was a member of a church and I had such a bad experience that I don't want to go through that again.

You yourself may have heard someone say:

4. I can't live up to every expectation, so I'm not willing to go through the formalities of belonging.

5. I like this congregation, but how do I know I would feel at home in other Free Methodist congregations if I should move? That's why I don't want to join a denominational church.

6. If I join, I fear I'll have to surrender some of my freedom in Christ.

Of course, there is one objection more difficult than most to acknowledge, but it is hidden in the feeling of some believers: I love Christ but what I see in the church is a different matter. Those who feel this way say, "Jesus, yes; the church, no."

We need to deal with these objections, but first, let us consider some reasons behind conflicts people have over belonging.

Ideas That Create Conflict over Belonging

I once came home from a trip abroad with an impressive collection of flea bites. I could not say where the little creatures had climbed aboard. So stealthy was their approach that I did not even know they had attached themselves to me. It was hours later that my conduct--subtle twitches in public, the shin-against-the-calf routine, monstrous scratching in the night--reflected their invasion.

In some ways ideas are like fleas. They may be abundant where people mingle, they pass from one to another unnoticed, and they have an ability to penetrate into our minds. Only later do we demonstrate their presence. Often we are at a loss to identify them or to know where it was they got aboard, but our conduct is different because of them.

Francis Schaeffer points out that we catch ideas like we catch measles--from our families and communities.

We live in a culture where ideas are plentiful and pushed.

Billboards along the highway, neons at night, subway posters underground, attractive magazines in planes aloft--there is no escape.

At home, in the evening, a half pound of freshly delivered newspaper awaits us on the front steps. Inside the house, color TV hypnotizes with news, sales pitches, sports spectaculars, documentaries, lottery drawings, and occasional religious appeals.

At the heart of it all are ideas, hundreds of them--some valuable, some worthless, some helpful, some damaging, some true, some false. But they all seek to win our allegiance.

And their abundance forces a constant sorting. Ideas that obviously conflict with Christian values are jettisoned. But not all ideas conflict *obviously*. Some seem harmless. Some have wide currency in our culture and we feel it a duty to host them. Others appeal to selfish impulses we have not yet had the courage to renounce. These ideas cunningly evade the sorting process.

This may account precisely for conflict we feel over belonging to the church. We go to services, participate in the fellowship, even serve and support. Obviously, there is some value in the church. But the thought of formally belonging triggers opposite feelings.

There are five ideas of great currency in our times that convey some measure of truth, but they lodge in our minds in such a way as to make us resist belonging to the church.

1. *"I want to do my own thing; I'm an individualist. I live in an individualistic culture and the church is an enemy to my freedom."*

It is true that we are more likely to reach our potentials for growth because we live in a culture that lays great stress on the individual. Individual worth, individual rights, individual initiatives, and individual tastes are integral to our way of thinking.

Test this idea. Suggest to an average group of high school students that every teenager should be required to wear a uniform to classes--or to an educator that all high school students should have to study algebra. Expect a reaction. "Everybody's different," you'll hear. You've obviously spoken against some fundamental principle by which modern life is regulated.

The emphasis on the uniqueness and worth of every individual is rooted in religion--some would say in the Judeo-Christian faith. And the encouragement of individual initiative accounts for certain dynamic qualities in our culture.

At the same time, if individualism flourishes, it downgrades both tradition and authority. Where traditions are highly honored, individualism must acknowledge limitations on its freedom. Where authority is respected--the authority of God, the nation, the home, the school--individualism can only have partial place.

This may be at the base of the conflict some Christians feel over belonging to the church. The church acknowledges some values out of the past, a fact it demonstrates in its traditions. And the church is inescapably committed to the recognition of authority; first the authority of God who is over all, and then the authority of His servants in church and secular structures.

The church, the structure in the world that celebrates Christ's concern for persons, may ironically be seen by the individualist as hampering individual initiatives and freedom. How can that help but stir conflict?

Add to this a sinful human desire we have all experienced to some degree--the desire for autonomy, total self-rule. Suzanne De Dietrich puts it into theological language thus: "Having lost our at-one-ness with God, we become like self-centered tops, turning round and round upon ourselves. We do this as individuals; we do it collectively on a world scale" (*The Witnessing Community*, Westminster, 1958, p. 23. Used by permission).

2. *"The church is an institution. Institutions are cold and uncaring. How can I belong to a body like that?"*

Institutions have come in for a beating in recent decades. Mammoth and faceless, they have been charged with robbing common people of personal worth. We have all had our bouts with unresponsive computers, and thousands know the sheer boredom of production lines. The consequent rage has contributed to sabotage, absenteeism, vandalism, thievery, and alcoholism.

This widespread antagonism to depersonalizing institutions, however, is not totally the result of personal experience. Ideas made current in the recent past have fed the antagonism.

The Romantics believed that evil was resident in institutions, not in individuals. Their flight from organized communities to unspoiled nature was a flight from evil. Soren Kierkegaard more than a century ago placed the individual ahead of any systems of thought and launched a withering attack on the Danish state church of his times. His attack has been taken up by many who don't even recognize his name.

These ideas have influenced us all, and some of us have grounded our decisions in them without even knowing it. The church, seen as an institution, therefore, raises feelings of conflict in us. It draws us because we sense God's people are there, but it also repels us because it is in some measure institutional.

Why can't the church be both a fellowship and an institution--a fellowship for the day-to-day needs of people and an institution for the ongoing needs of its ministry? If its task is to serve the poor and sustain missionary programs and support Christian colleges, some institutional means must be used to achieve these large goals.

The warmest churches I have known are churches that have accepted large challenges. I think of a congregation that contributed a total of $150,000 in one year and gave more than half of that amount to causes outside itself. You can't do that sort of thing by fellowship alone. But, if a baby became suddenly ill in the community, you could count on that church to surround the family with warm, caring love.

It is short-sighted to say, "Up with fellowship and down with institutions." Both have a place. If you need an emergency appendectomy, for example, you will not settle for the service of a fellowship. You'll be glad to have the operation supervised by an institution while you are gently coaxed and encouraged back to health by a fellowship. Let us have both, each in its place and both in one body.

   3. *"The church is too dogmatic. I believe everybody has to decide for himself what truths he will believe and what lifestyle he will adopt."*

New Christians don't often say this, but they feel it. In their pre-Christian lives they've seen claims to truth batted down often by the retort, "That's a matter of opinion." The discussion may be about common-law living or divorce or honesty--usually matters of morality.

It is one thing to say, "I have to decide for myself what truths I'll believe." We all must. It's another thing to say, "There are no absolute truths, only opinions." For those who hold the latter view, truth is a highly subjective matter. This position cannot help but make the church appear dogmatic. The church makes absolute claims for Christ and holds that the laws of God are unchanging in every age.

If this kind of subjectivism expresses your feelings, test it against the Ten Commandments in Exodus 20. Or measure it by the grand affirmations of Psalm 119. Or consider it after a careful reading of John 1:1-18.

A seatmate on a recent cross-country flight asked the stewardess for coffee as soon as we were aloft. This dapper businessman with a full, black mustache then proceeded to explain to me why he had done so. It was the end of a vacation period. He had been dancing until four o'clock that morning. The whole vacation had been spent in eating, drinking, and dancing, he said, and he had entered into each activity to offset the others.

When he learned I was a minister he switched nimbly to the subject of spiritual renewal in the church. With vigor he insisted that the new birth is the answer to people's deepest need. "The Spirit is being outpoured, and young people by the scores are being converted," he said.

He was an airplane salesman responsible for the sale of the wide-bodied Lockheed 1011 in which we were aloft. He spoke to me in fluent English and to the stewardess in easy French.

From the subject of church renewal, he moved to a miscellany of statements and opinions: Many Brahmins in India believe in Jesus Christ more than some Christians. Did I believe in reincarnation (that we come back to earth in a new form after death)? Some day all world religions will merge as a mark of progress. Billy Graham has suffered more illness since the death of Katherine Kuhlman, the faith healer.

His monologue was a verbal montage. He impressed me as one modern man who no longer believes that ideas should be consistent with each other nor that they need to be carefully examined. It seemed to me that I was getting a close-up of the damage subjectivism can do to the thought processes. He told me nothing of his personal life.

In spite of his religious fervor, he told me without embarrassment that he didn't belong to any church. He occasionally attended a large church near Los Angeles and spoke glowingly about it.

Subjectivism is an enemy to religious commitment of any binding sort. Besides, it is an enemy to moral uprightness and emotional stability. To the subjectivist, the church may seem dogmatic in its claims. But it's not dogmatic simply because it believes that truth is absolute.

    4. *"The church does not seem to be 'with it.' How can
       things written three thousand years ago speak to
       the issues that I face today?"*

If there is any one term that captures the complex ideological mood of our times, it is secular humanism. Humanism puts man at the center of the universe. But since there is a humanism which denies God and a humanism which can be called Christian, the word needs to be qualified. Hence, secular humanism.

Secular means worldly or temporal as distinguished from spiritual or eternal. When we refer to ideas as secular, we mean they pertain to the present age. The secular mind, then, is concerned principally with the here and now. The secular humanist is not likely to make an outright denial of God. He is more likely to say, "If God exists, it really doesn't matter."

You may have become a Christian by personal commitment to Jesus Christ, but your mind has not yet been reeducated to Christian values. Hence, belonging to the church is at least not of urgent concern and may seem quite unimportant. Could the reason be that secular humanistic values and the values the church represents are in conflict within you?

The church represents the eternal God. It has its roots in the ancient past, and its creeds make frequent references to the age to come. It is obviously not in tune with the secular humanist mind. The irony is, however, that those who take seriously the larger views of reality, held by the church, experience most richly the here and now. They handle the unresolved contradictions of life better, and their joy is more profound.

5. *"The church seems too intent on maintaining itself and not enough concerned with saving the world. It seems so halfhearted."*

New Christians, converted from the meaninglessness of our times, often get the impression that the church is out of touch with modern man's anguish. It seems to have everything buttoned down, and its concerns are largely for maintenance. They come to the church with a joy and spiritual passion, but the church, by its complacency, seems almost repelled by their joy.

It is true that churches, like people, get stiff as they get older. And congregations of people who have long since made their transition out of the world are in danger of forgetting what they have been saved from. The new convert sees this kind of church as placid, colorless, and lacking spiritual fervor.

But before you decide against belonging for this reason, consider: Does your congregation need the warmth of your new-found faith? Is it possible that in your fervor you have judged the church too severely, or before you have discovered the concerns that really are there? May their steadiness which bothers you be, in fact, the sort of ballast you need in these early days of your new faith?

Many congregations have become more like their culture than they realize. But God has not given up on them, and renewal is touching churches across the land. They are catching a fresh vision of the power of the gospel, the possibilities in Christian fellowship, and the worldwide mission of the church today. Besides, however you see the church, in the long pull you will fare more poorly without the church than with it.

Measure Ideas by the Bible

In examining the ideas that give us conflict over belonging to the church, one question stands ahead of all others: What does the Bible teach? Are these ideas in harmony with the Bible? God's Book surely must have a viewpoint on belonging.

To answer the questions, look briefly at three facts deeply imbedded in the Scriptures:

1. *Pentecost brought people together.*

Extreme individualism and anti-institutionalism divide

humans from one another. Look at our situation today. By contrast, the historic event of Pentecost, the birthday of the Christian church, brought people together. (Read Acts 2.)

Pentecost had a bridging and binding effect. The throng on that day represented many different languages, and language differences make for separation. Yet the gift of articulate speech enabled the throng to understand what was being said. A common message had a unifying effect.

Pentecost gave the disciples themselves a deepened sense of belonging. Peter was the inaugural spokesman on that day. But he did not stand alone. He spoke in company with the Eleven (v. 14). This sense of common purpose and mutual submission to one another had not always been the case for the apostles, the Gospels show.

And Pentecost marked a bridging and binding of the old dispensation with the new, even though it was a phenomenal event, unprecedented in history. Peter could have mustered good reason for presenting Pentecost as a beginning with no precedent. He could even have expressed contempt for all that was historical. He did not. Quoting the minor prophet Joel, he presented the inauguration of a new dispensation as a fulfillment of what had been prophesied in the old. (See Joel 2:28-32.) The two belonged to each other.

Finally, the young and the aged were put on a common footing at Pentecost--the old men dreaming dreams, the young men seeing visions. And sons and daughters were given equal notice, overturning discrimination by sex. Moreover, the lowliest in society--slave boys and girls--were acknowledged as belonging.

Not surprisingly, a mass conversion followed Peter's sermon on the Day of Pentecost. The hearers received Peter's word, believed, and were baptized, "and three thousand souls were added to their number that day" (v. 41).

How fully did they belong? "They devoted themselves to the apostles' teaching and to the fellowship, to the breaking of bread and to prayer" (v. 42).

The first converts discovered what it meant to belong. They were together. If our minds are colored by ideas that separate us from other Christians, especially Christians banded together by covenant and commitment, our ideas deserve testing. How do they measure up to the events of Pentecost? In the light of Pentecost, are such ideas a mark of spiritual health or spiritual ill health?

2. *We are members whether we acknowledge it or not.*

In a general sense, even the ruggedest individualists can scarcely escape belonging. They have memberships in unions or clubs, insurance programs, civic organizations, sororities, fraternities, political bodies, professional guilds, and so forth. However strongly we promote personal independence, our complex society survives on its collectivities. The person who feels resistance to church membership for individualistic reasons has the problem of achieving consistency.

It is true that membership in the church requires more by way of commitment than many other memberships do. But we must not forget that the big commitment is God's. He gave His very self in the event of Calvary and made the surrender unstintingly. In Jesus Christ, He bound himself to us that we might in turn be bound to Him and His people.

The idea of membership stems from Paul's comparison of the church to a human body. The parts of the church are members--hands, feet, eyes, ears--that individually serve the body. The body is an integral whole, but the members are many. Yet the one and the many are interconnected. Look at your hand to see how integral it is to your whole body. It is connected by bones, sinews, arteries, veins, nerves, muscles, and skin. Connected, it is a marvelous part of the whole and has a wonder of its own. Severed, it is grotesque and repulsive. We are made an integral part of Christ's body when we are converted to Him. Membership begins then. The church only asks us to register our membership--to belong in a specific place.

In the light of the Scriptures, belonging is a difficult thing to escape. To belong to Christ means to belong to His body on earth. Ideas that fill us with resistance to this reality must be seen for what they are--in some deep way, alien to God's purpose. The issue of church membership is simply registering with some body a membership God has already brought into being.

3. *God has always wanted to have a people--not just a person.*

Board a Boeing 737 at Cairo, Egypt, and fly eastward on the underside of modern Israel. If you don't see it first, the pilot may call your attention to it on the plane's intercom. There, to the south, in a vast stretch of unrelieved desert stands a mountain, stark in the distance. World famous still, it is the spot where the Ten Commandments were given by God. Its name--Mount Sinai.

The book of the Exodus gives the story in larger scope. A slave people, coming out of Egypt in droves, stopped at Sinai to regroup. Their leader, Moses, ascended the mountain to commune with the God who had delivered the slaves from the armies of Pharaoh. God made His presence known to Moses in a cloud. Before the people moved on from Sinai, God had entered into a pact with them. This agreement was called a covenant. (See Exodus 19-24.)

Here are the main features of the covenant:

1. *It was initiated by God, not by the people. It was He who made himself known, not they who discovered Him. On the basis of His mercy already shown to them, He invited them to enter, by covenant, into His Divine protection and service. This is called God's election (see Exodus 19:4).*

2. *The covenant established a bond between God and the people, giving them a special function in the world. "You will be for me a kingdom of priests and a holy nation" (Exodus 19:6). Priests are special to the god they serve. They have a special access to him and they come under his special care.*

3. *The covenant condition was that they were to live in obedience to God as a people. Jahweh was to be their king and they His subjects. They were to follow where he led (see Exodus 15:18; Deuteronomy 33:5). The Ten Commandments formed the basis for a life of national obedience.*

This event at Sinai illustrates a major fact about God's dealings. There is ample recognition of individuals in the Old

Testament. The book may speak about a man of God or a son of God or a prophet of God. But the dominant concern is with the people of God. We may call the Old Testament with equal accuracy the Old Covenant--God's covenant with a special people. Under the New Covenant, the special people is the church-- individuals collectively united in Christ for a common mission in the world.

Pentecost was marked by the recovery of true community. Members of Christ are members of His body in the world. God's covenant with Israel was a covenant with a people. Our problems over belonging to His church today must be evaluated in the light of these simple biblical facts.

Was Membership Less Complicated in Bible Times?

Some argue that membership in the church today is too complicated. For the New Testament church, conversion brought about automatic membership. Were not three thousand souls added on the Day of Pentecost?

The New Testament does not give us details on church life. We do not know what the early church did about membership records and courses of instruction. This could lead to the obser- vation that by our procedures today we have obscured the simplicity and spontaneity of belonging.

The argument is appealing but not thoroughly sound. In the Corinthian church, one member was living in sexual immorality. By letter, the Apostle Paul instructed the church to remove him from the fellowship and gave specific instructions on how this was to be done (1 Corinthians 5:1-5). This is the first record of an excommunication. In a later letter, further instructions were given on how this brother was to be restored (2 Corinthians 2:5-11). None of this could have been possible if membership, both for the brother and the congregation, had not been clearly defined and deeply important. Membership was obviously a less casual thing to early Christians than we might think.

The Cost of Belonging

Do some Christians feel resistance because of the cost of belonging? Perhaps, but not always because the cost is too high.

Elton E. Trueblood writes, "Many contemporary seekers cannot abide the church as they see it." In his opinion, the dissatisfaction "arises not from the fact that membership demands too much, but rather from the fact that the demands are too small" (*The Company of the Committed*, Harper, 1961, p. 9. Used by permission).

Membership in an organization that has a cross as one of its symbols and a sacrificial death at its center must be costly. Otherwise, it would invite people to live a lie. New Testament Christians paid a price for belonging, and so should we.

The Free Methodist Church wishes the cost to be consistent with the New Testament. We believe membership should call us to a threefold commitment: to Jesus Christ as Lord and Savior; to the company of His people with whom we identify here on earth; to the work He calls us to do in the world.

We acknowledge that a Christian has multiple obligations --to family, job, self, and community, as well as to the church. Our goal is to help every member to bring all commitments under one master commitment to Christ and His people. This can be done in such a way as to make all the other commitments more meaningful. Committed people are joyful people.

The Cost of Not Belonging

Those who have not yet come to terms with the cost of belonging should consider the alternative. Not belonging exacts a price too. Suppose you enjoy the fellowship of the church, you attend its services, you contribute to its ministries, but you do not wish to belong in terms of covenant membership.

As a result of not belonging, you may suffer from a feeling of inconsistency. You hold membership in other bodies--perhaps a union, a student body, or a professional society. You sign your name on the line for credit cards, bank accounts, insurance policies. In all these cases, you belong for mutual benefit. Some day you may wonder if it is consistent to belong to secular associations for the good mutually gained while refraining from belonging in at least as formal a way to a company of God's people.

Moreover, most Christians who participate in the church but refrain from membership are scarcely aware of the secular parallel to their mind-set. Growing numbers of people live in a relationship of marriage but refuse either to solemnize or legalize the relationship. How are the two attitudes essentially different? Both opt for benefits without a binding responsibility. This must be a costly contradiction to live with.

By not belonging you may increase instability for yourself or your family. A sixteen-year-old, wrestling with the question of values, for example, needs parents who have wholeheartedly identified themselves with Christ and His church. So does a nine-year-old who has given his heart to the Lord and has felt for the first time the desire to belong to the church. In fact, when the family faces crisis, the stability afforded by solid commitment to the church can be a decisive factor in how well the crisis is met. In such times, it costs to not belong. Single people need just as badly to belong. They need roots too. The church can be to them like an extended family, giving their lives greatly needed stability.

Finally, you may sense that by not belonging you are going counter to the New Testament. No one knew the weaknesses of the church of his day better than the Apostle Paul. The saints in Colossae were in peril of falling into heresy. Two sisters, Euodia and Syntyche, were in conflict in Philippi. Carnality and its consequences--strife, arrogance, childish conduct--were rife in the Corinthian church.

The Apostle Paul had every reason to hold himself aloof from these situations. Instead he prayed, wept, suffered, and taught as though he was dealing with his own dear children. There is never a suggestion that he felt like severing himself from the churches he was giving his life for. For better or for worse, he belonged.

If you reflect carefully on these costs (and others that might come to mind) you may conclude that the cost of not belonging is greater than the cost of belonging.

Benefits of Belonging

When we become active members of God's covenant people, benefits flow both ways. Recall the details of the covenant at Sinai. The people were to be the servants of God in the world, and through them His work was to be done. In them, the world was to have a true priesthood.

But the benefits flowed principally in the other way. As they kept the covenant, God was to be their protector. They were to have the benefits of living under His grace and sharing in the life of His human community. Consider some of the benefits that flow from belonging today.

You will have the satisfaction of knowing you are in harmony with the Scriptures. The early Christians became a part of the church as a natural and immediate step following their conversions. The whole mood of the New Testament is consistent with this fact. For example, when the disciples belonged to Jesus, they belonged to one another, even to the extent of having a common treasury. When Paul established churches, he organized them, setting elders over them. Baptism, the rite of belonging, is represented as a public event. When you enter wholeheartedly into the life of the church through a membership covenant today, you are in harmony with the whole tenor of Scriptures.

Belonging puts you in the position where you can affect the long-range ministries of a congregation. You are a voting member. You can feel free to offer your suggestions. You are eligible to participate in planning for the future. If God's blessing is poured out upon the energy expended, you will share in the warm sense of blessing that is sure to come down the road. If you go along only as an adherent, you are not so likely to share in the blessing.

By belonging you make a positive testimony to your family, the church, and the community. Consider what you say to your family when you offer yourself for membership. Whether they have joined ahead of you or not, you speak clearly of the depth of your intention. Consider what you say to the church itself. The step you take affirms them as a community. (If you withhold yourself from belonging, you are also making a statement to them.) And consider what you say to your community. In a world where spiritual values are precarious, you should take every opportunity you can to speak for God and His church.

The Free Methodist Approach to Belonging

Every church, whether independent or denominational, develops its own approach to membership. One church may require only baptism and profession of faith in Jesus Christ. Another may approach it by a course in the catechism or a confirmation class. The requirements for membership vary, as do the questions asked. Here is a brief outline of the approach the Free Methodist Church makes, as found in the *Book of Discipline*.

Youth Membership

Children are treated with warmth and care in a Free Methodist church. In accord with the example of Jesus Christ who took children on His knee and blessed them, we purpose to give them careful attention, leading them to a personal commitment to the Savior and opening the doors of the church to them. This is done by means of youth membership.

Members under sixteen years of age are asked to answer the following questions:

1. Do you believe that Jesus Christ has forgiven your sins and is now your Savior?

Answer: I do.

2. Have you received Christian baptism?

Answer: Yes or no.

   If not, will you consent to be baptized at such a time as your pastor may choose?

Answer: Yes.

3. Will you faithfully attend your pastor's class of instruction on living the Christian life and serving God through your church?

Answer: I will.

4. Will you be loyal to the Free Methodist Church and uphold it in your prayers, your presence, your gifts, and your service?

Answer: I will.

5. Will you endeavor to show your friends by your life what it means to be a Christian, and will you do your best to win them to Christ?

Answer: I will.

Preparatory Membership

For those communicants sixteen years of age and over, there are two levels of membership, preparatory and adult.

Preparatory membership is not covenantal. It is provided so that new converts may immediately receive the enfolding love of a community of faith and be given a sense of belonging. It is also provided to give the communicant opportunity to come to understand the nature and purpose of the Free Methodist Church before going on to the step of full membership. This is one way of manifesting our respect for the person considering membership.

When you enter preparatory membership, you will be enrolled in the pastor's membership class. Step by step you will study the basic doctrines, history, disciplines, and ministry of the church. Opportunity will be given you to ask questions, read further, and prayerfully consider whether the Lord is leading you into full participation in this fellowship.

Here are the four basic questions asked for preparatory membership. Anyone who answers these questions affirmatively is eligible for membership and will be warmly received.

1. Do you have the assurance that God has forgiven your sins through faith in Jesus Christ?

Answer: I have.

2. Are you willing to receive membership instruction as offered by our church?

Answer: I am.

3. Have you received Christian baptism?

Answer: Yes or no.

If not, will you receive this sacrament at a duly appointed time?

Answer: Yes.

4. You have been won to Christ. Will you endeavor to win others to Christ and the church?

Answer: I will.

Full Membership

When you have completed your pastor's membership class and been given opportunity to experience the love and concern of the congregation, you will move toward full membership. This may take place at any time after three months have elapsed from the time you became a preparatory member.

Full membership is based on a covenant. Upon your reception, you are eligible to participate in the life, administration, and ministries of the Free Methodist Church. It is an important step and we believe as you take it, guided by God, you will experience His blessing and the affirmation of the church. Here are the questions to be asked:

1. Have you now the assurance of the Holy Spirit that your sins are forgiven through faith in Jesus Christ?
2. Do you now experience the fullness of the Holy Spirit with His cleansing of heart and empowerment for service or if not will you seek His fullness through study, counsel, and prayer?
3. Do you intend to serve God by the full use of the abilities He has given you?
4. Do you believe the Holy Scriptures to be the revealed will of God containing all things necessary to salvation through faith in Jesus Christ?
5. Do you accept the Articles of Religion, the Membership Covenant, and the Organization and Government of the Free Methodist Church, and will you endeavor to live in harmony with them?
6. Will you, in fellowship with your pastor and fellow-members, avail yourself of the means of grace, such as, public worship of God, the ministry of the Word, the Lord's Supper, family and private prayer, and the searching of the Scriptures?
7. Will you practice the principles of Christian stewardship, giving freely of your time, talents and possessions to Christ and His church?

The Objections, Once Again

Early in the chapter, I listed common objections to belonging and promised I would return to them again. I do so now, in an attempt to show their size and importance,

1. *"I don't know how long I'll be living in this community."*

Church membership can be easily transferred, often more easily than bank accounts or other memberships. You may transfer to another Free Methodist church or, in a community where there is none, to another evangelical church. Then again, you may continue to live where you are now living for the next twenty years.

2. *"My loyalties are to another congregation or denomination."*

We all understand and appreciate loyalties. But we can use them as a way of living in the past or of shirking the loyalties that can motivate us to our best service in the present. Perhaps the finest way for you to honor your past in another church is to transfer your loyalties to the congregation of which God has now made you a part.

3. *"I had such a bad experience in a previous church where I held membership that I never want to go through that again."*

One can get hurt in the church because the church is made up of people who can make mistakes and sin against their brothers, sometimes without fully intending to. But if you are in a congregation now where you experience love, why withhold your love from this body because of something that is long past?

4. *"I can't live up to every expectation membership imposes."*

This is one of the hardest objections to deal with for these reasons: It is raised by some who are ardent Christians but who struggle with scrupulosity--the tendency to be overly rigorous about the smallest details. It is raised by others who really prefer an undemanding discipleship--a contradiction in terms--and who are therefore often on the lookout for loopholes.

If, after careful counsel with your pastor and prayerful self-examination, you are sure you are in the former category, always try to look past the statement of rules to the spirit that is behind them. God does not get glory from your perfectionism. He gets glory from your love for Him and His creatures.

If, on the other hand, you detect that you are the type of Christian who quickly seeks for reasons to sidestep any call to disciplined living, consider carefully the content and purpose of rules. They are meant to be aids to discipleship. You can become a more effective Christian by letting them challenge you to discipleship. And while you are doing so, thank God for a body that seeks to call its members to their best for the Lord.

5. *"I would feel fine about joining this congregation, but*

I'm not sure I want to belong to the whole denomination."

You could advance the same argument as a reason for refraining from being a registered citizen, too. But you don't. You judge your country as much by its highest ideals as by the ignorance or failures of a minority of its citizens. We ask you to think of the Free Methodist Church in terms of its vision and ideals for ministry.

6. *"If I join, I feel I will have to surrender some of my freedom."*

Human associations require some surrender. You have already done so by becoming a student at a university or an employee or a spouse or a parent. In fact, you have done so by becoming a human being. None of us has absolute freedom. To think we should have it is a myth of our times. The freest Christians are those who have internalized the ideals with which they identify. Then their lifestyle as Christians has a gracious freedom.

A Closing Word

If you know Jesus Christ as personal Savior, you are cordially invited into the membership of the Free Methodist Church. Whether you come into preparatory membership or have transferred from another evangelical body as a full member, we want you to sense that you belong. We'll help you to do so in any way we can.

Like Ken and Wanda, you may have stepped, arms wide open, into the church through which you had been led to faith in Jesus Christ. Or, like my newfound friends in Florida, you may have hesitated a long while for reasons you felt were sufficient. There may still be a sense of hesitation because your ideals of what the church should be are so far beyond what you perceive the church is where you live.

There is always a gap between the ideal and the actual--in the family, the business, the profession, the nation. We discover that gap within ourselves, too.

The committed member never surrenders his ideals about

the church, but he comes to terms with its shortcomings and human blemishes graciously. He practices the "love which covers a multitude of sins." The more he loves, the more ready he is to look for the best in the Christian brotherhood. "Love hopeth all things," refusing to take the failures he sees as final. He believes the grace of God will triumph in the fellowship--and in himself.

For Review:
1. What five current ideas bring conflict over belonging to the church?

2. What three scriptural facts answer the conflicts some may have over belonging to the church?

3. Outline the following in a three-column list: Cost of Belonging, Cost of Not Belonging, and Benefits of Belonging.

4. What are the three types of membership in a Free Methodist Church? Compare the questions asked of applicants for each type of membership.

For Further Thought:
In addition to those discussed in the chapter, what other answers can you think of to common objections to belonging?

God's new covenant is with His special people, the church. What is your responsibility and what is God's responsibility in this covenant?

CHAPTER TWO

Christian doctrine is what churches teach. The source book of Christian doctrine is the Bible, the raw material from which doctrine is organized. The purpose is to enrich your understanding, to give substance to your religious experience, to guard you from heresy, and to move you toward maturity in the faith.

Truths That Come First

If you are a new Christian, you have recently come alive to a great reality--God. What you have experienced is almost too moving to talk about: He loves you, He communicates with you, you can talk to Him personally, He cares what happens to you. More than that, you have learned there are other people who have similar experiences with Him. You have met some of them and when you are together, there is nothing like it: Christian fellowship.

If God is so real to you, what more do you need?

At first your answer is, nothing. That is, until you start asking questions: What is God really like? Can you see Him? When He is present at one place in the universe, is He absent from other places? Where is God when you don't feel His presence? What is His relationship to Jesus Christ? Does He love white people more than black people, or vice versa?

Ask a mellowed Christian these questions and you will get one sort of answer. From a Jehovah's Witness the answers will be subtly different.

So what do you do?

You have two alternatives. You can enjoy the spiritual experience and not worry about the questions. But if one of your newfound friends says that God loves all living humans and wants to save them and another replies that He loves only a select number He has chosen to love and has ordained that the rest should be eternally lost, you cannot just say, "Leave me alone and let me enjoy His presence."

This leads to the second alternative. You can try to understand what God is like and discover which of the above descriptions is most like Him.

As soon as you take this alternative, you have broached the matter of doctrine.

Christian doctrine is what churches teach. The source book of Christian doctrine is the Bible, the raw material from which doctrine is organized. The purpose is to enrich your understanding, to give substance to your religious experience, to guard you from heresy, and to move you toward maturity in the faith.

All the rest of your life you will be a student of Christian doctrine. You will want to develop a thoroughly Christian view of God, Jesus Christ, and the Holy Spirit and to wrestle with the wonder of the Trinity. You will never cease to ponder the doctrine of Creation. You will want to endorse the Christian view of man. The doctrine of the church will keep you stretching, and you will find challenge and comfort in the doctrine of the last things--how the world will end and the promise of God's heaven for the redeemed.

Some Christians worry that doctrine may become a substitute for spiritual life. They fear that knowing *about* God will take the place of knowing *God*. The danger does exist, and you should be on guard against it.

But there is as great a danger if you try to promote spiritual life without the help and guidance of doctrine. The Apostle Paul struck a right balance when he wrote to Titus: "But you must teach what agrees with sound doctrine" (Titus 2:1, TEV). *Sound* here means "healthy." The purpose of doctrine is to enhance the spiritual health of the Christian. It is life-giving.

Doctrine is as old as the Bible. It has always been a concern of the church; and from the start, Christian leaders have felt the need to systematize Christian beliefs. That is what doctrine is --systematized Christian truth.

In this chapter we will consider some basic doctrines for new Christians. These will be simple statements about Jesus Christ, His relationship to God, creation, redemption, the unknown future--and in all these, His relationship to you. We will call this a primer, and in these simple truths you will find food both for your mind and spirit. Doctrine is for the whole man.

Jesus Christ: History's Unique Human

History preserves the memory of many great humans: Plato, Beethoven, Shakespeare, Kagawa, Lincoln, Churchill. These towing personalities, the flowers of genius, come out of different cultures but belong to the whole race. Yet, when we get close to any one of them, our sense of awe abates slightly. Magnificent though their talents are, they are flawed humans.

Upon examining the heroes of our faith in the Bible, we come away with the same restrained praise. Abraham, David,

Solomon--they are remarkable humans and great in faith, but uniformly flawed. It is the truth about humans--with one exception. There was no flaw in Jesus Christ, history's unique human.

The Gospels make it clear that His was a human birth: "And she [Mary] gave birth to her firstborn, a son. She wrapped him in swaddling cloths and placed him in a manger, because there was no room for them in the inn" (Luke 2:7). Luke, a first-century physician, tells us that the birth of Jesus was the birth of a human baby into the human race. From the start, He was one of us.

Jesus developed and grew as a human. Concerning the long stretch from His infancy to His baptism when He was approximately thirty years of age, the Gospels are silent, except for one incident. At twelve years of age He visited the Temple in Jerusalem (Luke 2:41-51). Luke reports this event, noting that "Jesus grew in wisdom and stature, and in favor with God and men" (Luke 2:52). Jesus grew toward adulthood; that is, in His grasp of life, His physical development, and in His religious and social awareness. The Temple incident shows that at the age of twelve He was sensing a unique Sonship to God. At the same time, according to Luke's summary statement, He was experiencing a normal human growth toward adulthood.

Jesus experienced life as a human. During a time of exultation, He rejoiced (Luke 10:21); He became weary and needed to sleep (Matthew 8:24); on His cross He thirsted (John 19:28).

Jesus died as a human. He was crucified between two thieves and treated in all respects similarly to them (Luke 23:32, 33). His body was claimed and buried (Luke 23:52, 53). After He had yielded himself up to death, "one of the soldiers pierced Jesus' side with a spear, bringing forth a sudden flow of blood and water" (John 19:34).

The New Testament affirms Jesus' humanness in many ways. Eighty times He is called "the Son of man"; John refers to Him as the eternal Word who "became flesh" (1:14). Paul speaks of Him as "born of a woman" (Galatians 4:4) and of "being made in human likeness" (Philippians 2:7, 8). He was tempted (Matthew 4:3); He sweated (Luke 22:44); He was angry and grieved (Mark 3:4). Yet thoroughly human though He was, in one sense He was different from all other humans. He never once sinned.

He was flawless in character, we are told: "holy, innocent, undefiled, separated from sinners..." (Hebrews 7:26, NASB). He left himself open to possible humiliation by asking His enemies, "Can any of you prove me guilty of sin?" (John 8:46). None came forward with a charge. Those who knew Him best bore witness that He was a sinless human (1 Peter 2:22; 1 John 3:5; 2 Corinthians 5:21). In this respect, Jesus Christ was history's unique human.

Jesus Christ: God in a Human Body

The Scriptures clearly present Jesus as thoroughly human ("very man of very man," an ancient creed summarizes it) and at the same time as thoroughly divine ("very God of very God").

The Scriptures refer to Jesus as God. Of the eternal Word who became flesh, John says, "the Word was with God, and the Word was God" (John 1:1). Speaking of his own people, Israel, the Apostle Paul says, "Theirs are the patriarchs, and from them is traced the human ancestry of Christ, who is God over all, forever praised! Amen" (Romans 9:5).

Jesus is given divine titles. When the angel Gabriel revealed to the virgin Mary that she was to be the chosen bearer of a unique son, he promised, "He will be great, and will be called the Son of the Most High; ... and he will reign over the house of Jacob for ever; his kingdom will never end" (Luke 1:32,33).

To Him are ascribed the attributes of God. In the synagogue in Capernaum, the man with an unclean spirit cried out, "I know who you are--Holy One of God!" (Mark 1:24). Jesus did not rebuke him, accepting the statement and casting the unclean spirit from him. Moreover, God is regarded in Scripture as possessing wisdom without limit, and, in Christ, the Apostle Paul wrote daringly, "are hidden all the treasures of wisdom and knowledge" (Colossians 2:3).

Jesus' own claims are so outlandish that they must either be true or blasphemous. There can be no middle ground. "Anyone who has seen me has seen the Father," He told His anxious and perplexed disciple Philip (John 14:9). "I am in the Father and the Father is in me," He further claimed (John 14:11). "I am the way and the truth and the life. No one comes to the Father except through me," He told Thomas (John 14:6). When He said "I and the Father are one" (John 10:30), He did not mean one in purpose, as some claim, but one in being.

There are specific passages in the New Testament that summarize all the convictions of the early church that Jesus Christ was God in a human body. He was "in very nature God," Paul testified, and "did not consider equality with God something to be grasped." Yet He came "being made in human likeness" (Philippians 2:6, 7). Among the clearest claims are the words of the Apostle to the Colossians: "For in Christ all the fullness of the Deity lives in bodily form (Colossians 2:9) and "He is the image of the invisible God" (Colossians 1:15). That is, the eternal God is imaged forth in Jesus Christ visibly.

Jesus is therefore fully human and fully divine, the God-man who can represent God to us and us to God, participating fully in the natures of both. We can reflect on this--gain strength from it--but never fully grasp it. It is a part of the mystery of our faith.

Jesus Christ: The Agent of Creation

Little children getting their first science lessons find thoughts about the universe mind-bending. Where did it come from? How did it get to be here (or there, or here and there, or everywhere)? At some time or other we have all wrestled with these questions.

When we become Christians, the questions come back to us with renewed force. Is the God who has saved us a Creator God? Did He create everything?

The modern mind does not ask this question openly, but it pays a price for suppressing it. The novelist Theodore Dreiser wrote, "Life is to me too much of a welter and play of inscrutable forces to permit any significant comment. . . . As I see him, the unutterably infinitesimal individual weaves among the mysteries of a flosslike and wholly meaningless course--if course it be. In short, I catch no meaning from all I've seen, and pass quite as I came, confused and dismayed." In your pre-Christian days you may have had similar thoughts. If so, you need to consider the Christian doctrine of Creation.

The Christian faith tells us that God is the sole Creator of all that exists (Genesis 1:1). He brought it into being by the power of His own word. We may be troubled by the presence of evil, but we do not despair. Evil is not eternal: God is. This is His world. He sustains it and it exists for His glory. Disorder comes from revolt within His creation, not from some equally potent influence with which He must battle.

The New Testament holds that God created the world through Christ. "All things were made through him, and without him was not anything made that was made" (John 1:3). "By him," Paul writes, "all things were created: things in heaven and on earth, visible and invisible . . . all things were created by him and for him . . . in him all things hold together" (Colossians 1:16, 17).

This means that our Redeemer is our Creator. It means that human history from first to last is under the control and purpose of God as revealed in Jesus Christ. Beneath the disorder brought by sin, there is order created and sustained by God in Jesus Christ.

Jesus Christ: The World's Redeemer

Redemption is an important idea in the world of the Bible. If a man's slave passed out of his possession he might redeem him, paying a price for his return to his ownership. Redemption is a person's act of buying back something that formerly belonged to him but which for some reason had passed out of his possession.

It appears to the careful observer that the immediate world we move in has gotten out of God's hands. It's not the good place God intended it to be. Something has gone wrong. We ourselves give evidence of a bondage--real or potential--to some invisible force that seeks to dominate us. We need to be redeemed--taken back into God's possession in exchange for a price paid.

The New Testament teaches that Jesus paid that price and in doing so became the world's Redeemer. An important passage gives us His own words: "For even the Son of man did not come to be served, but to serve, and to give his life as a ransom for many" (Mark 10:45). This is matched by His further words, "I am the living bread . . . This bread is my flesh, which I will give for the life of the world" (John 6:51), and His pledge as the Good Shepherd to "[lay] down his life for the sheep" (John 10:11). In each case, redemption is implicit and a ransom paid to that end is in the foreground.

Jesus came to be the world's Redeemer. His redemptive act on Calvary was voluntary and costly and was carried out for those who could not redeem themselves. It stands in history as the one single and unique event in which mankind was redeemed back to God. The cost of this redemption is clearly the blood of Christ (Ephesians 1:7) and the provision is for the whole world (1 John 2:2).

The doctrine of redemption can save us from living our lives only at the level of our religious feelings. The price was paid, whatever our feelings say at any particular moment. This truth of redemption can also spur us to live lives of holiness and service. Twice, the Apostle Paul reminds his readers, "You are not your own; you were bought at a price. Therefore glorify God with your body" (1 Corinthians 6:19, 20).

Jesus Christ: Our Righteousness

Reflect on your own life for a few moments and you'll see that our days are filled with questions that demand answers: How much longer can I take the pressures at work? Can I keep ahead of the rising cost of living? Will I marry? Can we make our marriage work? What do people think of me, the way things have gone? Where can I turn for a job?

None of these is insignificant. But there is one question more fundamental and demanding than all these together, and it has universal scope. In the perspective of eternity, it's the most relevant of all: How can I get right and stay right with God?

In all the world, the question has only one of two answers. I may present to God a righteousness of my own, or I may declare myself incapable of such a feat and seek from Him a righteousness which He offers to give.

If I take the first course, I justify myself before Him by pointing to my good life or good deeds, pleading these as righteousness. If I take the second, I acknowledge that "all our righteousnesses are as filthy rags" flawed and soiled; and I declare personal bankruptcy, putting myself at God's mercy.

The latter is the Christian way. When we have no righteousness of our own to plead--and we acknowledge that fact--God offers us righteousness in Jesus Christ. He is "the Lord, our righteousness." The Apostle Paul spoke of this way of being put right with God when he wrote of wishing to "gain Christ and be found in him, not having a righteousness of my own that comes from the law, but that which is through faith in Christ--the righteousness that comes from God and is by faith" (Philippians 3:8, 9). In the Roman letter he makes reference several times to "the righteousness of God"--a righteousness which God gives in response to faith. Jesus Christ does not disperse this righteousness as a substance; He is this righteousness.

This great evangelical truth is hard, for several reasons, to appropriate. For one thing, the human heart is loath to acknowledge the inadequacy of the righteousness of man and the need for trusting wholly in Christ's righteousness. For another, some fear that the truth stated in this way will give grounds to shabby living. Those who propose it may say, "Christ is righteous, I don't need to be." In spite of problems like these, the truth that Jesus Christ is our righteousness is the foundation of Christian assurance and is a doctrine filled with comfort for the trusting heart.

Jesus Christ: Our Sanctification

God justifies sinners--in Christ. That is, through the merit of Christ's perfect sacrifice, He acquits sinners of their sins and permits them to stand before Him as though they had never sinned. Justification is a word from the language of the law court. It stands for a judicial act that deals in a judicial way with the wrongs committed against God's holy character. Full provision for our acquittal is made by Christ. We say, therefore, that Christ is our justification (Romans 5:1; 1 Corinthians 6:11).

God sanctifies those whom He justifies--in Christ. That is, He not only imputes to them His righteousness in justification, but at the same time, He begins to impart to them His own holy character in sanctification. Paul says, "Christ is made unto us ... sanctification" (1 Corinthians 1:30, KJV) and we are "sanctified in Christ Jesus" (1 Corinthians 1:2, KJV). William Burton Pope, an early Methodist theologian, wrote: "Christ is the scene, and sphere, and region, the temple, and shrine, and holiest, in which believers are consecrated and set apart."

The word sanctification belongs to the language of the Temple. Whom God acquits of sin He takes thoroughly into His possession and service. There is a large vocabulary related to sanctification: words like holy, holiness, saint, consecrated, devoted, set apart, and so forth. Sanctification begins in the moment we are forgiven. It involves process and crisis. It is both God's work and ours (2 Corinthians 6:1, 2), but it is ours only according to God's enablement. It encompasses the whole of the Christian life.

We cannot examine all these avenues of thought and experience in a primer such as this, but one thing must be clear at the outset: Sanctification is not something God dispenses to us separate from himself, like a doctor dispensing vitamins. Sanctification is what Christ is to us and in us and through us. It can never be separated from Him. In that sense, Jesus Christ is our sanctification.

Jesus Christ: Head of the Church

In the New Testament, the most common analogy for the church is the body of Christ. That is, it is more than an organization (though it will always have aspects of organization); it is an organism--a living, purposeful, growing entity on earth. To fill out the analogy, everybody needs a head, a unifying center of command; and Christ is the head of the church. God "appointed him to be head over everything of the church, which is his body, the fullness of him who fills everything in every way" (Ephesians 1:22,23).

This does not mean that we can disregard all human leadership and structures, out of deference to Christ's headship. The church is built upon the foundation of the apostles and prophets (Ephesians 2:20) and we show regard for Christ in our obedient attitude toward their teachings in the Bible. The church is provided by Christ with evangelists, pastors, and teachers (Ephesians 4:11) and we show deference to Him by respecting them as they proclaim and teach in His name (Hebrews 13:17). The headship of Christ over His church means that He gives order and vitality to all that is carried on in the church. He is the head. "From him the whole body, joined and held together by every supporting ligament, grows and builds itself up in love, as each part does its work" (Ephesians 4:16).

Jesus Christ: Lord of History

Read one line of truth separately in the New Testament and Jesus Christ will not appear to be the Lord of history. He was born in a cattle shed (Luke 2:7). He grew up in Nazareth, off the beaten track and in the modest home of a carpenter (Matthew 13:55). He lived a life of poverty (Luke 9:57, 58). In His most exalted moment He entered Jerusalem, not on a Roman charger but on a lowly donkey (Matthew 21:1-7), and He died the death of a condemned criminal (Matthew 27:38). This was all part of His humiliation.

Yet, over His head on the cross were posted the words, "This is Jesus, the King of the Jews" (Matthew 27:37). Meant for scorn, it is, ironically, a hint of a larger aspect of His person. He himself predicted, "When the Son of man comes in his glory, and all the angels with him, he will sit on his throne in heavenly glory. All the nations will be gathered before him" (Matthew 25:31-32).

After His resurrection and the inauguration of the Age of the Spirit at Pentecost, the young church saw Him as living Lord (Acts 2:36) and proclaimed Him so to the world.

The Apostle Paul set the humiliation and exaltation of Jesus together. Adapting words from Isaiah, he testified that "at the name of Jesus every knee should bow, in heaven and on earth and under the earth, and every tongue confess that Jesus Christ is Lord, to the glory of God the Father" (Philippians 2:10, 11).

At an appointed time, God will reveal to the whole universe that Jesus Christ is Lord. History itself will be shown to have bowed to His sway. That moment has not yet come, and many people live in the blindness of their unbelief. But Christians, though living in a world still under the prince of darkness, give daily testimony that the prince of darkness has already been judged and the lordship of Jesus is already affirmed. We await the coronation.

A Closing Word

When you *know* Christ firsthand by the help of the Holy Spirit, that's Christian experience. When you know *about* Christ through the teachings of the church, that's Christian doctrine.

Both are important to you. Doctrine without experience is

stuffy, pedantic, and often controversial. Experience without doctrine is whimsical and often divisive.

It is for reasons like these that the church has always tried to be definitive of doctrine. Across its whole history, you'll need creeds, articles, tracts, books, and sermons that have addressed themselves to the issue of good doctrine to keep experience on the track.

And for the same reasons, we confront you, a new Christian, with some basic truths about Jesus Christ. These can form a doctrinal foundation for your life. He is the alpha and omega of your faith.

Note: See glossary for definition of theological terms.

For Review:
1. What is doctrine?

2. List several things that were unique about Jesus as a human being.

3. What functions does Jesus perform as a divine being?

4. How are Christian doctrine and Christian experience related to each other?

For Further Reading:
> Demaray, Donald. *Basic Beliefs*. Grand Rapids, Michigan: Baker Book House, 1958. (Available from Light and Life Press.)

> Marston, L. R. *From Age to Age a Living Witness*. Winona Lake, Indiana: Light and Life Press, 1960. Chapter 16, "Doctrinal Integrity," and Chapter 17, "Christian Experience." (Light and life Press now located in Indianapolis, Indiana.)

For Further Thought:
What is the relationship between knowing about God and knowing God?

What is the Christian view of the nature, purpose, and destiny of man?

What is your view?

CHAPTER THREE

Our Articles of Religion are a part of the constitution of the Free Methodist Church. They tie us together as a people at deep levels. They come out of a common history, and, in an age too easily deceived into living life at the surface level, they give us greatly needed roots.

Articles of Religion may not flash with instant understanding like a Dear Abby column, but they have some things to add to life over the long pull that the most relevant newspaper column can never give. Keep this in mind as you consider them.

Truths That Unite Us

Since you are interested in belonging to the Free Methodist Church, you will want information on doctrine in wider perspective. What is the official position of the Free Methodist Church on major doctrines? How is our church related to historic Protestantism? Does it belong to the main stream or is it a side eddy? How does it stand on the great teachings of the Reformation?

You will also want to know the relationship of the Free Methodist Church to historic Methodism. How does our doctrine tie us to the evangelical awakening of the eighteenth century? This chapter will take up these questions, looking first at our Articles of Religion.

You may feel like ignoring the Articles of Religion. You can't understand them at a glance; they connect you with a history that is remote and uninteresting. Besides, how are they relevant to you where you live and work? Feelings like these are common these days, and I'm not surprised that you should have them.

But before you give in to such feelings, let me remind you that our Articles are a part of the constitution of the Free Methodist Church. They tie us together as a people at deep levels. They come out of a common history, and, in an age too easily deceived into living life at the surface level, they give us greatly needed roots.

Articles of Religion may not flash with instant understanding like a Dear Abby column but they have some things to add to life over the long pull that the most relevant newspaper column can never give. Keep this in mind as you consider them.

The Articles of Religion

On December 24, 1784, about eight years after the signing of the Declaration of Independence, sixty of the eighty-one Methodist preachers in the New World met in Baltimore, Maryland, to organize the Methodist Episcopal Church. Known as the Christmas Conference, this meeting marked the beginning of Methodism as a church. In England, recall, it had been only a movement seeking to work within a church. Now it was a denomination.

The conference adopted a discipline--a simple outline of instructions and orders--reflecting the general practices of Wesley and English Methodism. This discipline had two important features. It contained a liturgy revised by Wesley and referred to as the Sunday Service. It also contained Articles of Religion which outlined the teachings of Methodism on major points of Christian doctrine. The Sunday Service was soon replaced in the New World by more informal practices of worship, but the Articles of Religion were changed little until the General Conference of 1974.

Wesley had provided the new church with twenty-four articles of religion. These were a revision and simplification of the famous thirty-nine articles of the Church of England. The Christmas Conference added a twenty-fifth, "Of the Rulers of the United States of America." Thus, the Methodist Episcopal Church in America affirmed its doctrinal position in its twenty-five articles of religion.

When the Free Methodist Church was organized in 1860, slight revisions were made in the twenty-five articles. Three articles which referred to the heretical teachings of Rome were dropped. These had to do with the marriage of ministers, the taking of the sacrament, and purgatory. The article, "Of the Rulers of the United States of America," which the Christmas Conference had framed, was also dropped, along with one paragraph from the "Article on the Sacraments."

Two articles were added by the founders of the Free Methodist Church--Article XIII, "Of Entire Sanctification," and Article XIV, "Future Reward and Punishment." The former was composed largely of statements from Wesley's own writings and was intended to clarify the doctrine over which division had arisen in the parent church. The latter was added because the teaching of universalism (the belief that all people will ultimately be saved) was particularly strong in the mid-nineteenth century.

Articles of religion are limited in their purpose. They are not an exhaustive statement on doctrine. They are not for purposes of theological hairsplitting. But they do touch on essential points of Christian belief. They clarify Christian doctrine particularly at those points where it has been under the attack of heresy through the ages. They also form a brief summary of truth to guide those who are unable to study Christian doctrine exhaustively.

This thumbnail sketch gives evidence of the continuity of the Free Methodist Church with the Protestant Reformation, the religious awakening in England in the eighteenth century, and the formation of the Free Methodist Church of North America in 1860. The Articles of Religion were restated and updated at the General Conference of 1989. Before turning to these, you may wish to read the twenty-three historic articles printed in the historical index of the Discipline.

The Articles of Religion of 1989, are printed below:

THE CONSTITUTION: DOCTRINE AND MEMBERSHIP

A. ARTICLES OF RELIGION

GOD

I. *The Holy Trinity*

¶A/101.   There is but one living and true God, the maker and preserver of all things. And in the unity of this Godhead there are three persons: the Father, the Son, and the Holy Spirit. These three are one in eternity, deity, and purpose; everlasting, of infinite power, wisdom, and goodness.

II. *The Son*
His Incarnation

¶A/103.   God was himself in Jesus Christ to reconcile man to God. Conceived by the Holy Spirit, born of the Virgin Mary, He joined together the deity of God and the humanity of man. Jesus of Nazareth was God in human flesh, truly God and truly man. He came to save us. For us the Son of God suffered, was crucified, dead and buried. He poured out his life as a blameless sacrifice for our sin and transgressions. We gratefully acknowledge that he is our Savior, the one perfect mediator between God and man.

His Resurrection and Exaltation

¶A/104. Jesus Christ is risen victorious from the dead. His resurrected body became more glorious, not hindered by ordinary human limitations. Thus he ascended into heaven. There he sits as our exalted Lord at the right hand of God the Father, where he intercedes for us until all his enemies shall be brought into complete subjection, He will return to judge all men. Every knee will bow and every tongue confess Jesus Christ is Lord, to the glory of God the Father.

III. *The Holy Spirit*
His Person

¶A/105. The Holy Spirit is the third person of the Trinity. Proceeding from the Father and the Son, he is one with them, the eternal Godhead; equal in deity, majesty, and power. He is God effective in creation, in life, and in the church. The incarnation and ministry of Jesus Christ were accomplished by the Holy Spirit. He continues to reveal, interpret, and glorify the Son.

His Work in Salvation

¶A/106. We believe the Holy Spirit is the administrator of the salvation planned by the Father and provided by the Son's death, resurrection, and ascension. He is the effective agent in our conviction, regeneration, sanctification, and glorification. He is our Lord's ever-present self, indwelling, assuring, and enabling the believer.

His Relation to the Church

¶A/107. The Holy Spirit is poured out upon the church by the Father and the Son. He is the church's life and witnessing power. He bestows the love of God and makes real the lordship of Jesus Christ in the believer so that both His gifts of words and service may achieve the common good and build and increase the church. In relation to the world He is the Spirit of truth, and His instrument is the Word of God.

THE SCRIPTURES

IV. Authority

¶A/108. The Bible is God's written word, uniquely inspired by the Holy Spirit. It bears unerring witness to Jesus Christ, the living Word. As attested by the early church and subsequent councils, it is the trustworthy record of God's revelation, completely truthful in all it affirms. It has been faithfully preserved and proves itself true in human experience.

The Scriptures have come to us through human authors who wrote, as God moved them, in the languages and literary forms of their times. God continues, by the illumination of the Holy Spirit, to speak through this Word to each generation and culture.

The Bible has authority over all human life. It teaches the truth about God, His creation, His people, His one and only son, and the destiny of all mankind. It also teaches the way of salvation and the life of faith. Whatever is not found in the Bible or can not be proved by it is not to be required as an article of belief or as necessary to salvation.

V. Authority of the Old Testament

¶A/109. The Old Testament is not contrary to the New. Both Testaments bear witness to God's salvation in Christ; both speak of God's will for His people. The ancient laws for ceremonies and rites, and the civil precepts for the nation Israel are not necessarily binding on Christians today. But, on the example of Jesus we are obligated to obey the moral commandments of the Old Testament.

The books of the Old Testament are: Genesis, Exodus, Leviticus, Numbers, Deuteronomy, Joshua, Judges, Ruth, I Samuel, II Samuel, I Kings, II Kings, I Chronicles, II Chronicles, Ezra, Nehemiah, Esther, Job, Psalms, Proverbs, Ecclesiastes, The Song of Solomon, Isaiah, Jeremiah, Lamentations, Ezekiel,

Daniel, Hosea, Joel, Amos, Obadiah, Jonah, Micah, Nahum, Habakkuk, Zephaniah, Haggai, Zechariah, Malachi.

VI. *New Testament*

¶A/110. The New Testament fulfills and interprets the Old Testament. It is the record of the revelation of God in Jesus Christ and the Holy Spirit. It is God's final word regarding man, his sin, and his salvation, the world, and destiny.

The books of the New Testament are: Matthew, Mark, Luke, John, Acts, Romans, I Corinthians, II Corinthians, Galatians, Ephesians, Philippians, Colossians, I Thessalonians, II Thessalonians, I Timothy, II Timothy, Titus, Philemon, Hebrews, James, I Peter, II Peter, I John, II John, III John, Jude, Revelation.

MAN

VII. *A Free Moral Person*

¶A/111. God created man in His own image, innocent, morally free and responsible to choose between good and evil, right and wrong. By the sin of Adam, man as the offspring of Adam is corrupted in his very nature so that from birth he is inclined to sin. He is unable by his own strength and work to restore himself in right relationship with God and to merit eternal salvation. God, the Omnipotent, provides all the resources of the Trinity to make it possible for man to respond to His grace through faith in Jesus Christ as Savior and Lord. By God's grace and help man is enabled to do good works with a free will.

VIII. *Law of Life and Love*

¶A/112. God's law for all human life, personal and social, is expressed in two divine commands: Love the Lord God with all your heart, and love your neighbor as yourself. These commands reveal what is best for man in his relationship with God, persons, and society. They set forth the principles of human duty in both individual and social action. They recognize God as the only Sovereign. All men as created by Him and in His image have the same inherent rights regardless of sex, race, or color. Men should therefore give God absolute obedience in their individual, social, and political acts. They should strive to secure to everyone respect for his person, his rights, and his greatest happiness in the possession and exercise of the right within the moral law.

IX. Good Works

¶A/113. Good works are the fruit of faith in Jesus Christ, but works cannot save us from our sins nor from God's judgment. As expressions of Christian faith and love, our good works performed with reverence and humility are both acceptable and pleasing to God. However, good works do not earn God's grace.

SALVATION

X. Christ's Sacrifice

¶A/114. Christ offered once and for all the one perfect sacrifice for the sins of the whole world. No other satisfaction for sin is necessary; none other can atone.

XI. The New Life in Christ

¶A/115. A new life and a right relationship with God are made possible through the redemptive acts of God in Jesus Christ. God, by his Spirit, acts to impart new life and put us into a relationship with himself as we repent and our faith responds to his grace. Justification, regeneration, and adoption speak significantly to entrance into and continuance in the new life.

Justification

¶A/116. Justification is a legal term that emphasizes that by our new relationship in Jesus Christ we are in fact accounted righteous, being freed from both the guilt and the penalty of our sins.

Regeneration

¶A/117. Regeneration is a biological term which illustrates that by our new relationship in Christ we do in fact have a new life and a new spiritual nature capable of faith, love, and obedience to Christ Jesus as Lord. The believer is born again. He is a new creation. The old life is past; a new life is begun.

Adoption

¶A/118.   Adoption is a filial term full of warmth, love, and acceptance. It denotes that by our new relationship in Christ we have become His wanted children, freed from the mastery of both sin and Satan. The believer has the witness of the Spirit that he is a child of God.

XII. *Entire Sanctification*

¶A/119.   Entire sanctification to be that work of the Holy Spirit, subsequent to regeneration, by which the fully consecrated believer, upon exercise of faith in the atoning blood of Christ, is cleansed in that moment from all inward sin and empowered for service. The resulting relationship is attested by the witness of the Holy Spirit and is maintained by faith and obedience. Entire Sanctification enables the believer to love God with all his heart, soul, strength, and mind and his neighbor as himself, and it prepares him for greater growth in grace.

XIII. *Restoration*

¶A/120.   The Christian may be sustained in a growing relationship with Jesus as Savior and Lord. However, he may grieve the Holy Spirit in the relationships of life without returning to the dominion of sin. When he does, he must humbly accept the correction of the Holy Spirit, trust in the advocacy of Jesus, and mend his relationships.

The Christian can sin willfully and sever his relationship with Christ. Even so by repentance before God, forgiveness is granted and the relationship with Christ restored, for not every sin is the sin against the Holy Spirit and unpardonable. God's grace is sufficient for those who truly repent and, by his enabling, amend their lives. However, forgiveness does not give the believer liberty to sin and escape the consequences of sinning.

God has given responsibility and power to the church to restore a penitent believer through loving reproof, counsel, and acceptance.

THE CHURCH

XIV. The Church

¶A/121. The church is created by God; it is the people of God. Christ Jesus is its Lord and Head; the Holy Spirit is its life and power. It is both divine and human, heavenly and earthly, ideal and imperfect. It is an organism, not an unchanging institution. It exists to fulfill the purposes of God in Christ. It redemptively ministers to persons. Christ loved the church and gave himself for it that it should be holy and without blemish. The church is a fellowship of the redeemed and the redeeming, preaching the Word of God and administering the sacraments according to Christ's instruction. The Free Methodist Church purposes to be representative to what the church of Jesus Christ should be on earth. It therefore requires specific commitment regarding the faith and life of its members. In its requirements it seeks to honor Christ and obey the written Word of God.

XV. The Language of Worship

¶A/122. According to the Word of God and the custom of the early church, public worship and prayer and the administration of the sacraments should be in a language understood by the people. The Reformation applied this principle to provide for the use of the common language of the people. It is likewise clear that the Apostle Paul places the strongest emphasis upon rational and intelligible utterance in worship. We cannot endorse practices which plainly violate these scriptural principles.

XVI. The Holy Sacraments

¶A/123. Water baptism and the Lord's Supper are the sacraments of the church commanded by Christ. They are means of grace through faith, tokens of our profession of Christian faith, and signs of God's gracious ministry toward us. By them, he works within us to quicken, strengthen, and confirm our faith.

Baptism

¶A/124. Water baptism is a sacrament of the church, commanded by our Lord, signifying acceptance of the benefits of the atonement of Jesus Christ to be administered to believers, as declaration of their faith in Jesus Christ as Savior.

Baptism is a symbol of the new covenant of grace as circumcision was the symbol of the old covenant; and, since infants are recognized as being included in the atonement, we hold that they may be baptized upon the request of parents or guardians who shall give assurance for them of necessary Christian training. They shall be required to affirm the vow for themselves before being accepted into church membership.

The Lord's Supper

¶A/125. The Lord's Supper is a sacrament of our redemption by Christ's death. To those who rightly, worthily, and with faith receive it, the bread which we break is a partaking of the body of Christ; and likewise the cup of blessing is a partaking of the blood of Christ. The supper is also a sign of the love and unity that Christians have among themselves.

Christ, according to His promise, is really present in the sacrament. But His body is given, taken, and eaten only after a heavenly and spiritual manner. No change is effected in the element; the bread and wine are not literally the body and blood of Christ. Nor is the body and blood of Christ literally present with the elements. The elements are never to be considered objects of worship. The body of Christ is received and eaten in faith.

LAST THINGS

XVII. The Kingdom of God

¶A/126. The kingdom of God is a prominent Bible theme providing the Christian with both his task and hope. Jesus announced its presence. The kingdom is realized now as God's reign is established in the hearts and lives of believers.

The church, by its prayers, example, and proclamation of the gospel, is the appointed and appropriate instrument of God in building his kingdom.

But the kingdom is also future and is related to the return of Christ when judgment will fall upon the present order. The enemies of Christ will be subdued; the reign of God will be established; a total cosmic renewal which is both material and moral shall occur; and the hope of the redeemed will be fully realized.

XVIII. The Return of Christ

¶A/127. The return of Christ is certain and may occur at any moment. It is not given us to know the hour. At His return He will fulfill all prophecies concerning His final triumph over all evil. The believer's response is joyous expectation, watchfulness, readiness, and diligence.

XIX. Resurrection

¶A/128. There will be a bodily resurrection from the death of both the just and the unjust, they that have done good unto the resurrection of life; they that have done evil unto the resurrection of damnation. The resurrected body will be a spiritual body, but the person will be whole and identifiable. The resurrection of Christ is the guarantee of resurrection unto life to those who are in Him.

XX. Judgment

¶A/129. God has appointed a day in which He will Judge the world in righteousness in accordance with the gospel and men's deeds in this life.

XXI. Final Destiny

¶A/130. The eternal destiny of man is determined by God's grace and man's response, not by arbitrary decrees of God. For those who trust him and obediently follow Jesus as Savior and Lord, there is a heaven of eternal glory and the blessedness of Christ's presence. But for the finally impenitent there is a hell of eternal suffering and of separation from God.

Comments on the Articles of Religion

Every one of our Articles of Religion is rich in doctrinal

nourishment and could be properly studied in depth. But limitations of time and space require us to select only the following five for added comment.

GOD

I. The Holy Trinity

We believe in the one living and true God, the maker and preserver of all things. And in the unity of this Godhead there are three persons: the Father, the Son, and the Holy Spirit. These three are one in eternity, deity, and purpose; everlasting, of infinite power, wisdom, and goodness.

You may occasionally meet a person who rejects the doctrine of the Trinity because he does not understand it. He asks querulously: "God is three and God is one? Impossible!" He may be sincere, but he makes a mistake in rejecting whatever he cannot understand. His world is filled with things he can't understand--like love and water and space probes.

The doctrine of the Trinity belongs to the Christian mysteries. That does not mean it is incomprehensible; it means only that if we are to understand it at all, it must be revealed. Even then, our understanding is limited and we continue to hold it as a mystery.

Jesus' followers believed in God--a living and personal being who transcended all creation. They were taught to call this God, Father. But as those disciples looked at Jesus, heard His teachings, saw His miracles, and believed in His resurrection and ascension, they were convinced He was God. He was God in flesh, immanent in His world. Yet, they did not think they had met two separate gods. They had come to know one God, showing himself in two persons--God the Father and God the Son.

From the teachings of Jesus they learned also of the Holy Spirit (John 14:26). This Spirit then descended upon them on the day of Pentecost, filling them with boldness and power. He entered their lives individually and directed their fellowship corporately--from within. Far from showing himself as a mere force, He manifested attributes of personhood, giving counsel, rebuking, guiding missionary efforts. They came to understand that this too was God--God the Spirit.

So here was the mystery disclosed--God above us, transcendent; God among us, incarnate; God within us, immanent. All three persons of God disclose the same characteristics, and each is fully God. There are not three Gods, then, but one: one in three and three in one. That is what the word Trinity means: a tri-unity.

The doctrine of the trinity is no mere academic exercise. It is an orderly description of the reality every Christian may experience. If God were only above us, we might feel lost and lonely in His world. If He were only within us, we would have no way of distinguishing His will and directions from our own. If He had come into our humanity for only a brief life span, we would know what He was like then but have no continuing assurance of either His transcendence or His immanence. We need God in three persons--above us, among us, within us.

Consider some of the values of the doctrine of the Trinity First, this doctrine guides us in our experience of the one true God. Jesus said, "Anyone who has seen me has seen the Father" (John 14:9). Therefore, the highest thing we can say of the transcendent God is that He is like Christ. Jesus said, furthermore, "If anyone loves me, he will obey my teaching. My Father will love him, and we will come to him and make our home with him" (John 14:23). Here He is teaching that the Holy Spirit is the Spirit of God the Father and of God the Son. The doctrine of the Trinity, then, guides us in our experience of God, keeping us from wandering into error.

Second, this doctrine reflects our unity with the rest of the Christian world. You can find differences between Roman Catholics and Baptists or between Lutherans and Moravians, but not on the subject of the Trinity. All Christian bodies agree that God is one being who has made himself known in three persons without dividing the being or confusing the persons.

Third, the doctrine of the Trinity gives us a standard by which we may test false doctrine. The above article on the Trinity was first formed by the Augsburg Confession of 1530 to unify the German Reformers. But it was directed against Arianism, a heresy coming to the fore in the fourth century and teaching that the Son of God was not eternally existent with the Father but was rather one of His creatures. Arianism denied the Trinity.

A heresy that blossomed in the fourth century might seem irrelevant to the present if it were not that this heresy crops up again and again. The Jehovah's Witnesses in our times deny the Trinity, asserting that Jesus Christ is not one in being with the Father but only a creature of Jehovah God.

In reply to this and all other heresies denying the Trinity of God, our first article of religion affirms it. God is one, living and true. In the unity of God there is a Trinity of Persons. The three share an eternity of existence, a common deity, and a oneness of purpose. The triune God is everlasting, possesses infinite power, wisdom, and goodness.

The doctrine of the Trinity is encapsulated in the well-known Apostolic Benediction: "The grace of the Lord Jesus Christ, and the love of God, and the fellowship of the Holy Spirit be with you all" (2 Corinthians 13:14).

THE SCRIPTURES

IV. Authority

¶A/108. The Bible is God's written word, Uniquely inspired by the Holy Spirit. It bears unerring witness to Jesus Christ, the living Word. As attested by the early church and subsequent councils, it is the trustworthy record of God's revelation, completely truthful in all it affirms. It has been faithfully preserved and proves itself true in human experience.

The Scriptures have come to us through human authors who wrote, as God moved them, in the languages and literary forms of their times. God continues, by the illumination of the Holy Spirit, to speak through this Word to each generation and culture.

The Bible has authority over all human life. It teaches the truth about God, His creation, His people, His one and only son, and the destiny of all mankind. It also teaches the way of salvation and the life of faith. Whatever is not found in the Bible or can not be proved by it is not to be required as an article of belief or as necessary to salvation.

In the day-to-day life of the church and individuals, the focal issue is authority. Will the church and its members put themselves thoroughly under the Scriptures? Will they put themselves thoroughly under its direction in all things having to do with what one must believe and how one must live? Through the ages society has experienced moral upheavals and heard many false teachers. But the Bible is God's unchanging Word and final authority in matters concerning salvation and the life of faith.

SALVATION

XII. *Entire Sanctification*

Entire sanctification to be that work of the Holy Spirit, subsequent to regeneration, by which the fully consecrated believer, upon exercise of faith in the atoning blood of Christ, is cleansed in that moment from all inward sin and empowered for service. The resulting relationship is attested by the witness of the Holy Spirit and is maintained by faith and obedience. Entire sanctification enables the believer to love God with all his heart, soul, strength, and mind, and his neighbor as himself, and it prepares him for greater growth in grace.

Wesley emphasized the doctrine of entire sanctification to the point that it came to be called "the distinctive doctrine of Methodism." In any event, because of the centrality of the doctrine to Methodist thought and because of the conflict over the doctrine which figured in the organization of the Free Methodist Church, in 1860 the founders of our church added an article on this subject. They did so by putting together several statements of Wesley to present the salient features of the doctrine. In 1960, at the Centennial General Conference, the article was restated, not to change the doctrine but to give it greater clarity.

There is general agreement in all Christendom that only those who are fully cleansed from sin may enter heaven. But how and when is this full cleansing effected? In Roman Catholic teaching, the work of sanctification is completed by the fires of purgatory. In Calvinistic teachings, the work is generally declared to be finished in the hour of death. Methodism has taught that if the purification of the soul from sin is a work of God's grace, then it may be completed in this life in response to the consecration and faith of the believer. Article XII enlarges on this central teaching of historic Methodism.

LAST THINGS

XVII. *The Kingdom of God*

The kingdom of God is a prominent Bible theme providing the Christian with both his task and hope. Jesus announced its presence.

The kingdom is realized now as God's reign is established in the hearts and lives of believers.

The church, by its prayers, example, and proclamation of the gospel, is the appointed and appropriate instrument of God in building his kingdom.

But the kingdom is also future and is related to the return of Christ when judgment will fall upon the present order. The enemies of Christ will be subdued; the reign of God will be established; a total cosmic renewal which is both material and moral shall occur; and the hope of the redeemed will be fully realized.

The kingdom of God was not a large doctrinal issue in the days of the Protestant Reformation, and no article on the subject appeared in the major articles of the period. Consequently it was not dealt with in the historic 25 articles of the Methodist Episcopal Church nor the historic 23 articles of the Free Methodist Church.

But it is the central theme of the preaching of Jesus and the central fact confirmed by His miracles. In Jesus, that is, the kingdom of God had come among men. More than this, the kingdom of God embraces the total message of the Bible. Hence, in the 1974 reworking of our Articles of Religion, the General Conference approved the addition of an article on this subject, and the annual conferences with a more than two-thirds vote ratified it.

The kingdom of God means strictly the kingship or kingly rule of God. The term denotes the sovereign lordship of God over His people or over the world which He has made.

When a church assembles to worship, it affirms the sovereign rule of God over His people. When it meets to pray, it intercedes for the public manifestation of His lordship in the world. When it evangelizes, it seeks to extend the kingship of God over the lives of men. Institutions established by the church for educational or healing ministries or for the restoration of the sin-wounded give citizens of the kingdom opportunity to serve the King by serving His creatures in the world.

The reign that is now extending in spiritual ways, hidden from unbelieving eyes, will be revealed to the universe at the promised visible return of Jesus Christ. "Every knee [shall] bow

. . . and every tongue confess that Jesus Christ is Lord, to the glory of God the Father" (Philippians 2: 10, 11).

XVIII. The Return of Christ

The return of Christ is certain and may occur at any moment. It is not given us to know the hour. At His return He will fulfill all prophecies concerning His final triumph over all evil. The believer's response is joyous expectation, watchfulness, readiness, and diligence.

The doctrine of Christ's second appearing is as pronounced in the New Testament as the announcement of His first appearance.

Luke, for example, reports key facts surrounding the birth of Jesus Christ. He also records key events and teachings leading up to His death and resurrection. In his second account, the Acts of the Apostles, he describes Christ's ascension into heaven. Two men in white apparel are present to say to the disciples left behind, " 'Men of Galilee,' " they said, " ' why do you stand looking into heaven? This Jesus, who has been taken up from you into heaven, will come back in the same way as you have seen him go into heaven' " (Acts 1:11).

From that point on, the New Testament scriptures bear constant witness to this great Christian hope. Paul's first letter to the church in Thessalonica majors on the theme of Christ's return, a fact accented at the close of each of five chapters. Someone has calculated that one out of every 28 verses in the New Testament refers to the promise of Christ's return. It is the glorious hope set forth in the gospel and is a doctrine which gives force to the Christian evangel.

One scheme of Bible study known as dispensationalism divides human history into seven dispensations instead of the two in the Bible--the dispensation of Moses and of Christ. Following this, the dispensationalists develop an elaborate scheme of future events and, in a sense, calendarize the future in accordance with their interpretations of prophecy. This view of things, which came to prominence in the early nineteenth century, makes a strong appeal to those who accept its premises.

The Free Methodist Church, however, has never been drawn into dispensationalism as a way of interpreting Scripture. The present article underscores those emphases which are certain in the Scriptures: Jesus Christ will come again; His return is always immanent; the time is hidden from us; His return will mark a final and complete triumph over all evil; true believers expect this return and await it in watchfulness and diligent service.

Special Methodist Emphases

We have learned from our brief survey of the Articles of Religion that the Free Methodist Church is in the mainstream of Protestantism. But what is its doctrinal relationship to historic Methodism? The answer to this question can be drawn from a restatement of the major doctrinal emphases of historic Methodism.

Within the framework of Protestantism, the Methodist movement was raised up to stress certain evangelical truths. The three major emphases of the preaching of historic Methodism have been listed as follows: (1) All men may be saved, (2) All men may know that they are saved, and (3) All men may attain unto Christian perfection.

We may determine the doctrinal relationship of our church to the historic Methodist movement by considering these emphases.

All May Be Saved

This first doctrinal emphasis of historic Methodism pinpoints an issue which was crucial two centuries ago but is no longer intensely controversial today. Nevertheless, to appreciate the first of three distinctly Methodist emphases, it is necessary to consider the conflict in which it was rooted.

The issue was the doctrine of election, High Calvinism had vigorously held for unconditional election: From eternity past God chose to save certain individuals, and those individuals who were not chosen were elected to reprobation. The second half of the doctrine was not admitted freely by many who taught an unconditional election, but it logically sprang from the first. John Calvin in his Institutes admitted this when he wrote: "Some are foreordained to eternal life, others to eternal damnation."

Against this doctrine, the early Methodists asserted three

scripturally based propositions: That Christ died for all (2 Corinthians 5:14); that Christ is "the propitiation . . . for the sins of the whole world" (1 John 2:2, KJV); and that "he died for all, that those who live might live should no longer live for themselves but for him who died for them and was raised" (2 Corinthians 5:15).

One can see in these propositions an insistence upon an unlimited atonement, an atonement equal to the needs of all the sinners of the world and provided by God to be potentially effective in the lives of all. Methodism believed that the grace of God in Christ was freely offered to the whole world, and only those who excluded themselves by unbelief would be denied such grace.

The results of this emphasis were numerous: The gospel of Christ was offered to the poor, the downcast, the spiritually disfranchised. It was preached with great optimism and expectancy. None was excluded from the scope of its appeal. Hope was generated in the hearts of the hopeless. Methodist meetings became places of gladness and rejoicing. A hymnody which accented the theme of free grace developed and became a distinctive feature of the spreading revival. These results were related to the deep Methodist conviction that all men may be saved.

All May Know They Are Saved

The Holy Club of Oxford University in the late twenties of the eighteenth century was composed of men of piety and religious zeal but not men of Christian peace and joy. John Wesley, you will recall, made a heroic trip to the New World to teach Christianity to the Indians, but he returned with the awareness that he himself had never been inwardly converted to God. Thus, for 12 years he was both an ordained priest of the Church of England and a searcher after inward peace.

This search came to its conclusion on May 24, 1738. Back in London after his New World adventure, he had met Peter Bohler, the Moravian, who had showed him that salvation is by simple faith in Christ and not by the accumulation of good works. The truth began to find its mark. John Wesley records his own personal conversion which took place on May 24, 1738.

In the evening I went very unwillingly to a society in Aldersgate Street, where one was reading Luther's preface to the

Epistle to the Romans. About a quarter before nine, while he was describing the change which God works in the heart through faith in Christ, I felt my heart strangely warmed. I felt I did trust in Christ, Christ alone for salvation: and an assurance was given me, that he had taken away my sins, even mine, and saved me from the law of sin and death.

This was one of the outstanding spiritual events of the eighteenth century. A crystallized doctrine of unconditional election had discouraged the teaching of personal assurance. If God's choices were locked up from human understanding in His inscrutable councils, how could one be sure? Unbelievers and believers alike were left uncertain, and any claim to inward Christian assurance was immediately branded as fanaticism. John Wesley's personal conversion, attended as it was by a sense of Christian sonship, marked a turning point.

Under the preaching of the Wesleys, Whitefield, and other preachers who followed, the experience of personal assurance became increasingly common. Conversions were attended by joy and inner peace. Converts testified to a deep awareness that God had forgiven them and adopted them into sonship. The witness of the Spirit, a term based on such passages as Romans 8:16 and Galatians 4:6-7, became common in the vocabularies of preachers and laymen alike. Methodism proclaimed with certainty that all men may know that they are saved.

This second major emphasis of historic Methodism does not seem novel in our generation since the truth has become an essential part of all evangelicalism. Nonetheless, it remains an identifying mark of the preaching of genuine Methodism, and its counterpart in Christian experience is the birthright of every convert to the Christian faith. To this, the Free Methodist Church heartily subscribes.

All May Experience Christian Perfection

In every age, there have been Christians who have taken note of the language of perfection in the New Testament and have seriously set their goals according to it. Some have shot high, and some wide of the mark. But in all Christian centuries there have been those who have taken the subject seriously.

It is safe to say that no one addressed the matter more earnestly or persistently than John Wesley of the eighteenth century. His distinctive contribution to the understanding of this subject is twofold. He taught that the perfection to which the New Testament points believers is a perfection of love and that it is a perfection open not merely to monks hidden away in cells or to Christians of a very select sort but to all who will set their sights resolutely in this direction.

What are some of the Scriptures that give grounds for a doctrine of Christian perfection? Consider our Lord's words at the center of the Sermon on the Mount: "Be perfect, therefore, as your heavenly Father is perfect" (Matthew 5:48). In another instance, Paul wrote to the Philippian Christians: "Let us therefore, as many as be perfect, be thus minded" (Philippians 3:15a, KJV). In the latter case, the perfect were those who single-mindedly pressed toward a yet higher perfection which could be realized only after the resurrection of the body (v. 11).

Evidently, they were in one sense perfect while in another sense imperfect--a paradox of perfection which Methodist theology has freely acknowledged. This paradox underlies the qualifying of the term "perfection" by the adjective "Christian." At another point in the New Testament, Hebrew Christians, who were floundering spiritually and in danger of being drawn back into Judaism, were exhorted: "Therefore leaving the principles of the doctrine of Christ, let us go on unto perfection" (Hebrews 6:1a, KJV).

So runs the language of perfection through the New Testament. The very word for perfection used in each of the above cases occurs with arresting frequency. As the adjective "perfect," it appears no less than 17 times; as a noun "perfection," twice; and as a verb "to perfect," it occurs 14 times. And in the New Testament the related ideas of the single eye (Matthew 6:22) and the call to blamelessness are given (Philippians 1:10). Historic Methodism has rightly given the doctrine of Christian perfection a central place in its message, and this teaching has been appropriately called the "last and crowning doctrine" of Methodism.

What is the perfection the Christian may know? It is the

perfection of his love to God and his fellowman, a teaching amply set forth in the New Testament. For example, when Jesus said, in the Sermon on the Mount, "Be perfect, therefore as your heavenly Father is perfect" (Matthew 5:48), the perfection of God to which he refers is reflected in God's love for all men. The Christian goal is no more and no less.

The same is set forth in Jesus' enunciation of the basic commandments: "Love the Lord your God with all your heart and with all your soul and with all your mind. This is the first and great commandment. And the second is like it: Love your neighbor as yourself " (Matthew 22:37-39). Historic Methodism has sought to set this imperative before its people as an attainable goal because God commands it.

The doctrine of Christian perfection, however, has not been free of pitfalls. Some who have preached it with zeal have claimed for it more than the Scriptures warrant, setting before Christians goals unattainable in this life. Nor have all exponents of the doctrine reflected the love and humility so central to it.

On occasion the doctrine has been pressed upon hearers in such a way as to make earnest Christians feel guilty if they could not yet profess to have been perfected in love. Only those Christians who are not seeking to obtain the gift of perfect love should feel guilt. But misdirected zeal has sometimes put the added burden of guilt on those who, seeing the goal, were pressing toward it, but for some reason had not yet come to the assurance that God's love fully governed their hearts.

On yet other occasions, the doctrine of Christian perfection has been isolated from the great biblical truth of justification by faith. Article IX of our historical twenty-three articles reads: "We are accounted righteous before God only for the merit of our Lord and Savior Jesus Christ by faith, and not for our own works or deservings; wherefore, that we are justified by faith only is a most wholesome doctrine, and very full of comfort." No other doctrine of Scriptures is to obscure or replace this truth, foundational to all others.

If seekers after Christian perfection lose sight of the fact that they are "accounted righteous before God only for the merit of our Lord and Savior Jesus Christ," they may unconsciously come to regard the quest for Christian perfection as an effort for salvation by works. At times when the doctrine has been under particularly severe attack, this latter error may well have made an appearance. It is the error from which the Wesleys were delivered.

These errors notwithstanding, the Christian goal is love "out of a pure heart, and of a good conscience, and of faith unfeigned" (1 Timothy 1:5, KJV). To set our sights on less is sub-Christian. The genius of the Methodist movement was the steadiness with which this goal was held before all believers. Historic Methodism believed that all Christians may attain unto Christian perfection and therefore all Christians should unswervingly seek to do so. This belief remains a doctrinal emphasis of the Free Methodist Church.

A Closing Word

My wife and I were driving north on Bay Street in Toronto one chilly fall night recently. Tall buildings stood like giant sentinels on either side of us, but the street was remarkably quiet. We had driven downtown at the close of the day to look and talk.

I broke the silence to ask, "What difference would it make to our lives if we didn't believe any of the Christian truths we hold dear--truths about God and man and salvation and the world to come?"

Perhaps it was the wonders of the modern city that had teased the question to the fore. We were driving along a corridor of architectural wonders. Maybe it was prompted by contradictory thoughts about secular man--he's so brilliant and at the same time so wicked. He believes so little about ultimate matters.

"Our lifestyle is largely fixed now," I said. "If our religious beliefs were suddenly canceled out, would our lives actually change?"

My wife's first response in the quietness of the car was, "Not much."

Then, after reflection, she said with a smile, "Maybe we wouldn't be so careful about not telling little white lies." It was a half-humorous response.

We turned left on Bloor and headed homeward, exploring the question further as we eased from traffic light to traffic light.

Before the matter dropped we had come to a surprising agreement. There would be changes--subtle but real ones. We would lose the ground for our joy. Besides, our home and our budget and our use of time and our associations would all change. Some things might change more than we anticipated. Who could say in advance all that would change?

The doctrines of the Christian faith, devoutly held, are bedrock to a lifestyle that is pleasing to God and distinctive in the world.

Note: See glossary for definition of theological terms.

For Review:

1.   Trace the history of our historic 23 articles of religion back to the Church of England,

2.   List the six major headings under which our current 22 articles of religion are organized.

3.   How does the doctrine of the Trinity minister to your Christian life?

4.   In what ways may the doctrine of the kingdom of God be more clearly reflected in the life of your church?

5.   What are the three major preaching emphases of historic Methodism?

For Further Reading:

Binney, Amos, and Steele, Daniel. *Binney's Theological Compend.* New York, Nashville: Abingdon Press, 1902.

Wesley, John. *A Plain Account of Christian Perfection.* London: The Epworth Press, 1952.

Hymnal for Worship & Celebration, "Hymnal of the Free Methodist Church." Word Music, Irving, Texas 1989 (especially hymns by Charles Wesley).

The Faith and Life of a Free Methodist. Winona Lake, Indiana: Light and Life Press, 1976. (Light and Life Press now located in Indianapolis, Indiana.)

Pamphlet: *Doctrinal Patterns*. Winona Lake, Indiana: Light and Life Press. (Light and Life Press now located in Indianapolis, Indiana.)

My Church Brochure Series: *What Is a Free Methodist?* and *Walking in from left and right*. Winona Lake, Indiana, Light and Life Press. (Light and Life Press now located in Indianapolis, Indiana.)

For Further Thought:

How may doctrine be used more effectively for Christian nurture in your church?

Which of the three major emphases of historic Methodist preaching is most in need of recovery in the church today? Consider ways this emphasis could be renewed.

See Paragraph 131, *The Book of Discipline*, 1989 for appropriate scriptural passages.

CHAPTER FOUR

The apostles were witnesses because they had firsthand knowledge of the facts concerning Jesus, His life, death, and resurrection. They passed these facts along in spoken and written form together with the elaboration of a total lifestyle which was stimulated by these facts. The church today is in league with them because the Holy Spirit makes every generation of believers contemporary with Christ. The Holy Spirit gives us a firsthand certainty of Christ's life, death, and resurrection. That is, the New Testament bears testimony to this, and the Holy Spirit confirms the reality to us in personal experience.

Witnessing To Grow

Let me tell you about Church X. It's a Free Methodist congregation whose attractive pale salmon brick facilities are located toward the eastern edge of a dense urban population. The area is made up of two adjacent cities which together boast a population of more than 230,000 people. The area is industrial and the major product is General Motors cars.

Attend Church X on an average Sunday morning. Stay through the two services and the Sunday school hour. You'll see 360 people gather from all directions. The usual number of young families will be noticeable. Go to the crib room in the newly built education wing and you'll look in on a growing infant population. You'll find the worship services warm, inviting, and people caught up in what they're doing. Fellowship after service will be animated and pleasant. You'll want to return.

What makes Church X seem like a wonder of God's grace is that only fifteen years ago the dozen or so people who formed the backbone of the struggling congregation were hard pressed to know what to do. They had sold their old property. They could not seem to find land on which to build. Trying to hold things together, they were meeting in a school that was sometimes cold and dingy. Should they trudge on or call it quits.

How did Church X get from that state of affairs to their present vibrant and outward-reaching stance? It would be easy to credit the pastor who first lead them out of the wilderness or the pastor who followed him. It would be easy to give accolades to the present senior pastor and his two assistants. They are all deserving. Each has made a large contribution. Moreover, churches never grow beyond the vision of their pastors. Even so, Church X is not a pastor-owned church. And to credit exclusively any or all of these valiant workers would be to oversimplify the miracle of God's grace in this remarkable church.

Ask the present senior pastor what the key to this pulsating, growing phenomenon is and he'll tell you things like this: "We're a witnessing church. We emphasize lifestyle evangelism. We have regular seminars on this method and we attempt to get all our people into one. Lifestyle evangelism is our main thrust."

But then he'll continue, wanting to be sure you get an accurate picture. The following facts tumble forth one after another: lay pastoral visitors take their faith into nursing homes and hospitals. Some members share their faith in the workplace. The people expect to hear reports of conversions from week to week. In fact, if too many weeks pass and the backlighted cross in the chancel remains unlighted (meaning no one has been converted that week) people get concerned, prayers intensify and questions begin to form.

The enthusiasm of the pastor of Church X rises noticeably when he talks about worship services. In these services, he explains, people experience the presence of God. New persons coming into the congregation notice the difference. They want to come back. This congregation is learning increasingly to practice the presence of God and this makes them a really caring people.

You may be a new Christian reached by the witness of another Christian, or a believer who has come to the Free Methodist Church in search of a vital fellowship. You may be a long-time member taking a refresher course and at this time in your life seeking spiritual renewal. Whichever you are, you have a right to ask about the Church X story: Is this the result of gimmickry? Are leaders compromising to get people in? Will it last, or is it another flash in the pan? Church X, like many other Free Methodist Churches in North America, is simply trying to be a witnessing church, and it's growing. Not all growing churches are healthy churches, but healthy churches are growing churches.

Some Biblical Facts About Witnessing

The New Testament Church Was a Witnessing Church

In the days immediately after Christ's resurrection, what was the church like? Was it daring or defensive? Was it unified by some central mission that shaped its very life, or was it one more sociological body that took its cues from its communities? Where did Jesus fit into the picture? New Christians will want to consider the matter of witnessing and growing with some thoroughness, and the starting place is the New Testament.

The young church described in the Acts of the Apostles bore

witness to Jesus Christ as resurrected from death, and hence as Lord over His people. He was central to their faith. That's what Peter proclaimed on the day of Pentecost (Acts 2:14-36). Moreover, this was the issue the antagonistic rulers raised when they first hailed the apostles to stand before them, "We gave you strict orders not to teach in this name . . . Yet you have filled Jerusalem with your teaching and are determined to make us guilty of this man's blood" (Acts 5:28). Later, the persecution that broke out after Stephen's martyrdom dispersed Christians in all directions. It was a cruel blow, but "those who had been scattered preached the word wherever they went" (Acts 8:4).

All this is significant for several reasons. First, the Acts of the Apostles is the first historical account of the Christian church. It is an inspired document and so can be trusted to show us what the church was like in its earliest days. It was above all else, a witnessing church. Second, this document follows an outline arising from words spoken by the resurrected Lord: "You will receive power when the Holy Spirit comes on you; and you will be my witnesses in Jerusalem, and in all Judea and Samaria, and to the ends of the earth" (Acts 1:8). Quite simply, this was a commission to bear witness to Jesus--everywhere.

The book of Acts does not stand alone in this accent on bearing witness to Jesus Christ. The Gospel according to John is a document with a distinctive emphasis on witnessing. The word "witness" occurs 34 times as a verb and 13 times as a noun. This total of 47 references contrasts with a total of 16 in the other three Gospels. The Acts of the Apostles makes clear and the Gospel of John reinforces the fact that the Christian witness is not first of all to certain doctrines or certain modes of life. It is a witness to Jesus Christ as God incarnate and resurrected from death.

Let us take just one example, citing John 5:29-40. The chapter reports first that Jesus healed a man at the pool near the sheep gate in Jerusalem. The Jews were enraged and filled with murderous thoughts because Jesus had broken the Sabbath and called God His Father. In the resulting dialogue between the Jews and Jesus, He spoke of a fourfold witness to His divine person: John the Baptist bore witness to Him (v. 32); His own works bore witness (v. 36); the Father himself who sent Him bore witness (v. 37); and the Scriptures the devout Jews so carefully studied bore witness (v. 39).

All this from the Acts and John make one thing clear, and we can apply it to our witness today. Our commission is not so much to bear witness to salvation as to Jesus, the one who saves. If we lose sight of this simple fact, our witness can be hurt. For example, it can so easily degenerate into talk of subjective religious experiences--of a wide variety.

Bearing witness to Jesus will not obscure the fact of salvation. When one trusts his whole being to Jesus Christ, he is saved and made conscious of salvation. But the experience of salvation is in a sense reflexive. That is: the gospel is about Jesus Christ; the Scriptures bear witness to Jesus Christ; and saving faith is faith in Jesus Christ. The person whose faith is wholeheartedly in Jesus Christ will have the deepest personal sense of salvation. It is to Christ, therefore, that witness must be borne.

Consider our spiritual forebears. The eighteenth century Methodists bore witness to Jesus Christ formally in their preaching and informally in their conversations. This witness was supplemented by good deeds, unconsciously extended by disciplined and holy lives, and brought home to a surrounding society by the caring fellowships that formed. It is in the history of the Free Methodist Church, rooted both in the Scriptures and the Methodist revival, to be a witnessing people--bearing testimony to Jesus Christ as Savior and Lord.

Witnessing Is Every Christian's Business

A zealous but troubled Christian layman from New York State recently asked me a very direct question. It sounded to him as if the church was saying that witnessing is the task of a select number--perhaps preachers and a few brave and gifted laymen --but the majority of Christians in the church do not have any obligations to be witnesses. He wanted to know if he was hearing it correctly. His urgent question deserves an answer.

Among the Apostle Paul's closing exhortations to the church at Colossae is this word: "Be tactful with those who are not Christians and be sure you make the best use of your time with them. Talk to them agreeably and with a flavor of wit, and try to fit your answers to the needs of each one" (Colossians 4:5, 6, *Jerusalem Bible*). From this one passage, it is obvious that Paul did not intend the Christian faith to be verbalized by preachers only. It was an assignment for every member of the church.

Talk . . . with a flavor of wit? Consider a sidelight on the Apostle's instruction.

What Christians said to non-Christians was always to be "seasoned with salt" (NIV). It was to be "never insipid" according to the *New English Bible*. The *Jerusalem Bible* paraphrases Paul's exhortation: "Talk (to those who are not Christians) agreeably and with a flavor of wit." In classical writings before New Testament times, salt was used as a metaphor for the knowledge or wit with which conversation was seasoned.

Today, wit means humorous or clever speech. It has not always had that meaning. Actually, wit is a fairly old root for knowledge. This appears in the *King James Version* of the Bible where it occurs in different tenses. Of Moses, coming down from a time of extended communion with God, the KJV says, he *wist* not that his face shone. This is a form of the verb "to wit."

Generally speaking, the verb has disappeared from modern English. But, in the word "witness" it continues as a part of our language. A witness is someone who has firsthand knowledge.

The apostles were witnesses because they had firsthand knowledge of the facts concerning Jesus, His life, death, and resurrection. They passed these facts along in spoken and written form together with the elaboration of a total lifestyle which was stimulated by these facts. The church today is in league with them because the Holy Spirit makes every generation of believers contemporary with Christ. The Holy Spirit gives us a firsthand certainty of Christ's life, death, and resurrection. That is, the New Testament bears testimony to this, and the Holy Spirit confirms the reality to us in personal experience.

Therefore, every generation of Christians is to be a generation of witnesses. Every church is a part of God's witnessing community. The Christian witness may be adapted in special cases, as when the evangelist moves from witnessing to the active winning of converts. The pastor too may fulfill a specialized role, since he is exhorted to "do the work of an evangelist." But broadly speaking, witnessing is not a specialized task of a specialized class of workers. It is an assignment to every Christian.

The Witness of the Church Today

Consider several aspects of the witness of our church today.

1. Free Methodist congregations, when they are at their best, give forth *informal and spontaneous witness* to Jesus Christ. The pastor of one of our fastest-growing churches, reported on a city-wide interdenominational program to train Christians to communicate their faith to non-Christians in a saturation effort. You might guess that his laymen were involved in great numbers.

Two hundred fifteen members of this congregation took part in the training and the visitation that followed. The pastor reported later that his first concern was not to garner a host of new members through this effort but to see his people involved in informal and spontaneous witness. "The important thing to me," he said, "is that for these people, witnessing has now become a way of life."

A witness, you will recall, is someone who has firsthand knowledge. In everyday life it may be knowledge of a robbery or a wedding. A Christian witness has firsthand knowledge, too, and is willing to speak up. The knowledge of a Christian witness is that Jesus Christ is alive and makes His saving presence known to all who put their faith in Him. That's something to talk about--informally and spontaneously.

2. Free Methodist churches at their best also make a place for *organized witness*. This means recruits are enlisted (usually for home visitation) and training is given. Then at least a night a week is set aside so the visitors can martial their courage and support one another, keeping at the task. At the close of an evening of calling, reports are made. The calling secretary keeps records, and follow-up calls are planned. Professions of faith are noted and steps are taken to involve the new converts in the nurturing fellowship of a warm, caring church. The church then assigns sponsors to keep in touch with new Christians.

Those churches which incorporate this aspect of witnessing --a combination of witnessing and evangelism--into their ongoing life know what an exacting ministry it is. Recruits come slowly. It is a weekly discipline that faces uncommon obstacles. A pastor and church board succeed only when they feel the force of the Great Commission within themselves and make the ministry a priority matter in all church programming. This is the feature of modern church life most resisted by the kingdom of darkness.

At the same time, those Christians who resolutely participate experience joy. They see the spiritual needs of modern man firsthand. They sense in others, often to their surprise, a hungry response to the Savior to whom they bear witness. Sunday worship takes on vitality for them because they expect visitors or newfound converts to be there. Their own prayers are vitalized. Best of all, they experience the living presence of Jesus Christ who commissioned them to be His witnesses. To those who are, He promised, "Lo, I am with you always, even unto the end of the world" (Matthew 28:20, KJV).

There is a place in the life of Christians, then, for spontaneous witness and for organized witness as well. But these do not exhaust all the possibilities.

3. Consider what might be called a *supplemental witness* to Jesus Christ. This is the witness of good works. We do not do good works in Christ's name in the hope that they will improve our chances to be saved. That is, they are not done to win merit with God. It is important to know that all merit for our salvation is in Jesus Christ who justifies us freely before God in response to our faith in Him. Good works follow, not to clinch our salvation, but to give evidence of it (Ephesians 2:8-10). Good works are acts of obedience and gestures of love.

Consider the works of a little-known disciple named Tabitha who lived at Joppa, the seaport of Jerusalem about 39 miles to its northwest (Acts 9:36-42). When this woman fell ill and died, the Christian community was stirred with grief and sent for Peter, known to be about ten miles away.

Death that robs the ranks of a Christian fellowship always has its sad aspect, but the Joppa fellowship was peculiarly stirred by this death. Tabitha was much loved for her ministrations to the widows. She had sewn tunics and cloaks for them--inner and outer garments--and this demonstration of good works was its own kind of witness to the saviorhood and lordship of Jesus Christ. Peter, in an incident similar to Jesus' raising of Jairus's daughter, performed a miracle in restoring Tabitha to life. She was then presented to "the saints and widows."

Here in one brief narrative we are exposed to several features of the life of the early church. There was a vital fellowship. One disciple was noted not for her preaching but for her good works. The Christian community was visited by the miracle-working power of God. Yet, with all this, the focus of the church was not blurred. The end result was that "many believed in the Lord." The good works were obviously supplemental to the spoken witness the community bore to Jesus Christ.

There are many references in the New Testament to the importance of good works. We are saved "unto good works, which God hath before ordained that we should walk in them" (Ephesians 2:10, KJV). This is what the Apostle Paul taught the Ephesian church. Earlier, in the midst of vigorous doctrinal discussion, the pillars of the church in Jerusalem gave Paul and Barnabas the right hand of fellowship, sending them to bear witness to the Gentiles. Paul adds that the pillars of the church reminded them to "remember the poor, the very thing I was eager to do" (Galatians 2:10).

All this should not be surprising. Jesus himself had said that a cup of cold water given in His name would not go unrewarded. Moreover, His great parable of judgment, the separation of the sheep from the goats, set as a basis for distinction not words spoken but deeds done: I was sick and you visited me. I was hungry and you fed me (see Matthew 25:35-36).

The verbal witness to Jesus Christ, whether spontaneous or carefully organized, goes poorly unless in the congregation there is an overflow of good works. It goes no better where good works have become a substitute for verbal witness. But where good works are supplemental to the spoken witness, the world gets a multidimensional message and the work of the Lord prospers.

There are Christians like Tabitha in the church today. One quiet Christian whom I knew personally, retired from her regular employment as a teacher and asked her pastor for visitation assignments. From that day on, for several years, she called on a growing number of shut-ins, taking some to the grocery store, reading to others, and doing whatever she could to minister to them in Jesus' name. Only yesterday a young business man in one of our churches reported to me that he and his wife had taken into their home a young, unemployed Christian. They intend to help him find work and become established in a job.

Every Free Methodist church has a board of stewards, or they may be incorporated into the organization of the official board. In the early days of the Methodist revival in England, the stewards cared for and dispensed the funds of the growing societies. Much later, they were given the additional task of preparing the elements of the Lord's Supper. In recent times, the board of stewards has been assigned more comprehensive duties in caring for the needy, comforting the sick, serving the aged, and so forth. (See 1989 *Book of Discipline*, ¶A/404.5.) The *Book of Discipline* is in harmony with the early church, however. It concludes that the board of stewards is to keep in mind "that all of its services have but one objective, the redemption of the soul in a full knowledge of Jesus Christ."

Nothing must blunt the central witness of the church.

4. Undergirding spontaneous, organized, and supplemental witness, Free Methodist Christians at their best bear an *unconscious witness* to the saving power of Jesus Christ. From the start they are called to take seriously not only God 's free and gracious offer of the forgiveness of sins but also His call to holiness of heart and life. Holy people--saints--are never conscious of their own holiness, but their lives take on a quality which the world cannot help but notice.

Strictly speaking, Christians never do have a holiness of their own. Holiness is, first of all, an attribute of God. "I am holy," the Lord said to Moses as He made himself known to him. Only then did He follow to say, "Be ye therefore holy."

In one sense, holiness is an indefinable word. We know it suggests something about the "otherness" of God and His blinding splendor and purity. We know also that the more closely His people associate with Him, the more His holiness is seen through them. This is Christian holiness.

Holiness, of course, can be caricatured. It can be pictured as eccentric or strange. Such misconceptions of holiness make it seem abhorrent to reasonable people. The Pharisees displayed a self-conscious holiness that drew this sort of response.

Even so, it is a mark of historic Methodist teaching that there is a holiness of heart and life to which the New Testament calls believers. Holiness of heart suggests that, at the center of one's being, Jesus Christ rules in the power of the Holy Spirit. Holiness of life suggests that, as a consequence, one's daily walk increasingly reflects Christ's kind of concerns and conduct at the personal, family, and social levels.

The New Testament calls believers to this quality of life (Romans 6:13; 12:1, 2). In doing so, it indicates that one does not automatically begin there. It further reflects that a believer can suffer from arrested development and settle for being a carnal Christian (1 Corinthians 3:1). But the norm is full sanctification (1 Thessalonians 5:23, 24).

The life of full sanctification is a life of constant dependence on the power of the Holy Spirit, who is the sanctifier. It is a life lived in the fellowship of the church. It is never marked by a constancy of emotion (emotions are changeable and subject to many external influences), but it is characterized by a constancy of will. In its ethical aspect, it is manifested by love for God and man. It is personal in the sense that it is lived devotionally. It is social in that it is marked by a growing concern to meet the needs of one's fellowman.

This quality of spirituality is attractive to many people outside of Christ. It is therefore an unconscious witness to the possibilities Jesus Christ holds out to His followers.

Witnessing and Growing

To the above four dimensions of Christian witness, we add a fifth. The Free Methodist Church at it best also bears a *corporate witness* to Jesus Christ. It may seem to you a small thing, but when a congregation gathers with disciplined regularity for worship at an appointed meeting place, the people say something to their community about the hold Christ has upon their loyalties. A parking lot, filled with cars on a Sunday night, witnesses mutely to those returning from a day of secular pursuits. The sight may say something to passersby who have been ignoring their hunger for God. The same can happen on a midweek night.

When our people show a simple love for one another, this too is a part of their corporate witness. The love is sensed by visitors who are there when the church is meeting. But in an average community, even those who stay at a distance come to know about it. Jesus said this would happen. "By this all men will know that you are my disciples, if you love one another" (John 13:35). Christ's kind of love cannot long be kept hidden.

The corporate witness of the church has many elements. Christian families, for example, stand out in a community. One woman moved into a small midwestern city. Of Jewish parents, she had not been accustomed to attending church. After a few weeks she came to the Free Methodist pastor's study with two of her children to ask permission to bring her family to church. She had met three families from the church, she said, and they all showed qualities she wanted her children to have. They seemed so respectful of each other.

Add to these elements the integrity with which members of the church conduct their business affairs. Add the support they show one another in times of distress or tragedy. Include the church programs which contribute to the well-being of the community. All these make the church like a corporate light set on a hill, pointing those who see it to Jesus Christ, the church's Savior and Lord.

The witnessing church can never exist merely to maintain itself. Some churches slip into this kind of existence, but it is a repudiation of the Great Commission. When any church is in harmony with God's purpose for it, everything it does is related to its witness to Christ in the world.

Practical Matters Regarding Witnessing and Growing

This leads us to consider some practical and contemporary matters with respect to witnessing and growing. What is distinctive about churches that are witnessing and growing today? I asked half a dozen pastors of growing churches some questions. Here are a few of the answers.

In your opinion, what should new Christians do to contribute to the witness and growth of the church they are joining?

1. One minister said simply: "Let them get involved in some type of ministry." (You may have to let your pastor know of your interest and ask him to have the nominating committee consider where you might serve best.)

2. "The new Christian needs to get into a Bible study, new membership class, or some other group where he will be nurtured in the Scriptures," another minister replied. (This pastor implied that the new Christian must ground his faith in the Word of God at the same time he is seeking opportunity for ministry.)

3. One pastor replied: "We get new Christians into a weekday growth group as our denomination recommends and into a discipleship Sunday school class for three months. In this they learn the basics of the Christian life. Then they are graduated into a three-month-long membership class. But right from the start, we urge them to share their newfound faith with neighbors and friends."

4. The pastor of a large church that has been growing for several years wrote: "We expect a new convert to become involved in Christian ministry, and we start from the beginning to train him for it. We also urge him from the start to be loyal to the gatherings of his church--making attendance a wholesome habit."

All pastors agreed that new Christians have a faith to nurture and to share, and the witnessing and growing church makes training and new experiences in Christ possible.

How many of your members are involved in assigned ministries that take them outside the walls of the church--hospital visitation, jail visitation, home visitation to share the gospel, home Bible studies, and so forth?

1. One pastor of a growing church with one hundred sixty-five members reported that thirty-eight members of his congregation take part in the following community ministries: (1) jail visitation twice a week, (2) regular Bible studies with "dry" alcoholics, (3) regular lay visitation of shut-ins, (4) regular Tuesday night evangelistic home visitation, (5) between five to seven regular weekly home Bible studies.

2. Another replied that 10 percent of his membership is involved in bus ministry, outreach visitation of families (at least three calls per month), and home Bible studies that begin anew every six weeks.

3. A pastor of a medium-sized church that has gained seventy-five members in the past five years reported that between 15 and 20 percent of his membership carry on assigned ministries outside the church building. These include nursing home ministries, bus ministry, home visitation, and home Bible studies. He added that many Sunday school teachers visit their class members or prospective class members during the week. As well, a specially trained team of six couples serve as class leaders and assist the pastor in his own pastoral calling ministry.

It's apparent that growing churches have many forms of witnessing to their faith in Jesus Christ and of taking that witness into the community. But none was without an evangelistic ministry in which they skillfully and forthrightly invited people to receive Jesus Christ and become a part of His church in the world.

What does your church do in your community to bear witness to Jesus Christ--either corporately or individually?

1. One said: "I have members who serve on the school board, and several are members of civic clubs. Some of my men are businessmen and they are known for their integrity. I have several women who are involved in community women's groups, both secular and religious. They are not shy about their faith.

2. A pastor reports that his church has become so visible in the whole city that he was appointed by the governor to represent the Protestants in his state for the bicentennial celebration.

3. "Our church cares for people who hurt, and our city of 30,000 knows it," another pastor answered, "but it's not just emotional or physical hurts we minister to. We care for people who need Christ."

4. The pastor of a small but growing church says: "Some of our members participate in Telecare (Telephone Christian Listening Service). But we are doing our best work through Sunday school outreach and home visitation."

A Closing Word

When a pastor and his congregation look toward becoming a witnessing and growing church, there are perils to be avoided. Consider two.

There is the peril of defining witnessing too narrowly. If witnessing comes only to mean evangelizing, a nucleus of Christians may be zealous to win commitments to Jesus Christ without developing a growing church into which to welcome them. When the church is growing as God intends, it grows in worship, service, good works, and community--a multiple witness to the grace of Jesus Christ. But defined too narrowly, witnessing may only mean a home visitation program or a bus ministry or periodic evangelistic series. The church that falls into this sort of error will only reduce witnessing to a fad and long-range good will be limited.

There is the opposite peril of defining witnessing too broadly. The church that falls into this error may develop programs and carry on a variety of activities. It may provide workers for the blood bank, participate in community religious services, rally support when emergencies strike either within or outside the congregation, send visitors to the retirement homes, and otherwise make its presence felt. But if these activities are not undergirded by a forceful statement of the gospel, the witness to Jesus Christ as Savior and Lord will lack transforming force.

The first peril may lead to a much too exclusive emphasis on evangelism. The second may produce an active community which, for all its activities, never rejoices over the saving of the lost. The church which God approves has a balance between worship and ministry, prayer and good works, fellowship and community concern, nurture and evangelism. And, as the result of the wholesome witness it bears to Jesus Christ, it has an evangelistic growing edge. Witness to Him unifies everything else.

If you wonder how common people can witness, let me tell you about a conversation I had with a pastor. After a luncheon together, I was about to get out of his car to enter my host's home. Before doing so, I asked, "Do you have Christians in your church who witness for Jesus Christ spontaneously in their daily lives?"

He told me about a jet pilot and instructor in the air force. The instructor had recently been sent to a community one hundred miles distant to make a presentation to a group of air force personnel. As the evening progressed, he noticed a woman officer who seemed troubled. The instructor sat down across from her during coffee break and she began to give the reasons for her distress. Things were not going well at home.

When the right time came, the instructor told her simply that he had once been in the same state, but he and his wife had turned to God and asked for His help. The woman was open to his words so he went on and told her about Jesus Christ. Before he left to return to his base that night, she had made a very elementary commitment to Jesus Christ.

Next morning, back home, he phoned his pastor. Giving him the account, he then told him that the woman would be in the nine o'clock service next Sunday. She was coming to spend the day with him and his wife. She came that Sunday and the next. During the third week, the pastor referred her to an evangelical church in her own town.

Your church will give you more detailed instruction on the ministry of witnessing. But there is a way you can get started. At the outset of each day--starting tomorrow--pray for at least one opportunity to share your faith in Christ. Then, be alert. God will give the opportunity because this is the kind of prayer He loves to answer.

For Review:
1. The Christian is to bear witness to whom? To what about this person is the Christian to bear witness?

2. What are several biblical suggestions for the witnessing style Christians should use?
3. Identify and explain five aspects of a local church's witness.

4. What should new Christians do to contribute to the witness and growth of the church they are joining?

For Further Reading:
Your pastor can direct you to books and materials that would be helpful to you. Also your church publishing house, Light and Life Press, Indianapolis, IN, can recommend recent publications for you to read and use.

For Further Thought:
Think of an associate at your place of employment. How can you improve your personal witness to him?

What should your church do to improve its witness?

CHAPTER FIVE

There is an inclination today to brush church history aside as though it were unimportant. This gesture is so subtle as to be scarcely recognizable, even to the person doing it. One may say, "Let us be concerned with what is relevant to the present"--as though history were not. Another, "Let us talk about what God is doing today"--as though you can tell without the perspective of history.

History That Is Valuable

"Why do we have to study this junk?" a sixth grader asked at the beginning of a history lesson.

The teacher was ready for him. "How would you like to live without your memory?" she asked. Then she began to show him what it would be like.

He would forget who he was, where he lived, that he had parents, the taste of apple pie, what happens when you touch a cactus, and all the fun he had had the day before.

When his eyes grew sober with understanding, his teacher said, "History is not junk. It is the memory of the human race."

Church history, a specialized branch of the larger field, is the memory of the Christian church. Even so, there is an inclination today to brush church history aside as though it were unimportant. This gesture is so subtle as to be scarcely recognizable, even to the person doing it. One may say, "Let us be concerned with what is relevant to the present"--as though history were not. Another, "Let us talk about what God is doing today"--as though you can tell without the perspective of history.

They are capital ideas, mind you, but not as alternatives to the serious consideration of history. They are only helpful reminders to keep the study of history from becoming stuffy and remote.

If we are indifferent to our history, we can't escape being narrow-minded. To put it another way, living in ignorance of our history is like living in a house without windows.

The object of this chapter is to point out certain reference points in the history of the Free Methodist Church. The chapter is more an outline than a detailed statement, and if your appetite is whetted you will need to turn to larger volumes.

What is noted here is considered necessary to help you experience mature belonging. Maturity, as a person or as a Christian, involves some awareness of preceding generations. Adolescents, for example, may be sufficiently caught up in self-discovery as to disregard those generations that have preceded theirs; but it is a sign they are becoming mature when they feel the need for the backward as well as the forward view.

The questions before us in this chapter are simple: Where did the Free Methodist Church come from? Why does it exist?

The Church of England

The Christian church probably came to England during the second century of the Christian era. During the Middle Ages, like the rest of Christendom, it came under the domination of Rome. But by the eighteenth century, it had become a clearly organized state church known as the Church of England, with a well-defined theology, a distinctive organization, and a properly constituted clergy.

We cannot here trace in detail the evolution of the Church of England. But in passing, we can note some of the major events that made it into the church it had become by the beginning of the eighteenth century.

The Official Break with Rome

We are well aware, of course, that the Protestant Reformation took place in sixteenth-century Europe and that the revolt of Henry VIII of England against the church of Rome was an important step in the coming of that event to England. His revolt was brought on by his desire to have his marriage to Catharine of Aragon annulled. Whatever the reasons for the thwarting of this desire by the Pope, Henry was declared to be "Supreme Head of the Church of England," by an act of Parliament in 1534, and the breach with Rome was official.

The church in England was set free from Rome by this action, but the separation was largely political. The pre-Reformation atmosphere persisted in the churches of England. Two centuries later, great changes had taken place. To account for these changes, we must consider at least two more important events.

The Thirty-nine Articles

In 1571, the famous Thirty-nine Articles of faith were adopted as the doctrinal standard of the state church in England. These were Calvinistic in flavor, but they did commit the church to a Protestant theology. They have remained to the present day the official statement of doctrine for the Church of England. Thus, we must regard the adoption of these articles in 1571 as an important factor in the shaping of the Church of England.

The Puritan Effort to Reform the Church

About the time of the adoption of the Thirty-nine Articles, a corps of English clergymen began a concerted effort to purge their church of the remnants of Roman superstition. They strongly renounced the elaborate attire worn by the clergy and objected to the sign of the cross at baptism as mere superstition. Their opposition to these and other medieval practices and their efforts to purge them from the church soon earned for them the title "Puritans."

By 1660, one hundred years later, the Puritan movement had reached its climax. Even though it had made sweeping changes by parliamentary legislation, it could not sustain the changes. Consequently, when the monarchy was restored, the Church of England was returned to the rule of bishops and the *Book of Common Prayer* was established again as the official guide for the liturgy of the church.

Then reaction set in. At least two thousand ministers who were unwilling to adhere to the worship and government of the restored state church were ejected from their churches. Legislation was enacted making it illegal for them to hold services. The church and the country thus suffered an incalculable loss, for among these persecuted Puritans were some of England's most godly clergymen.

The Early Eighteenth Century

The reaction which set in showed itself not only in a series of legislative acts intended to stamp out dissenters but also in a general moral collapse. Puritanism had been strict. Now a wild orgy of immorality swept the aristocracy of the country, fanning out until it had corrupted every level of society. Of the morals of early eighteenth-century clergy and laity, Bishop Berkeley wrote in 1738: "Morality and religion have collapsed to a degree that has never been known in any Christian country."

In those early years of the century, the church was ruled by bishops who lived as lavishly as princes. All too many of England's parsons were known for their drinking excesses and indulgence in sports. At the same time the church was served by a greater number of clergy who half starved on less than fifty pounds a year. Advancement came through political preferment. And the prevailing mood of the church as a whole was one of skepticism.

The state of society was correspondingly pitiful. Coarse literature was the vogue. Theater was dissolute, so decadent it cast rogues in the role of heroes and made noble characters the butt of jokes. Drunkenness was pervasive and violence so common that one took his life in his hands when he went out alone in the cities.

Immorality was regarded as normal, and sexual promiscuity filled the towns with illegitimate children. Public hangings took on a carnival spirit. The historians of the age bear witness to all this. It is tragic that in it all, the Church was so much a part of the age that it had very little to offer.

Summary
We have surveyed rapidly some of the major factors that shaped the Church of England of the eighteenth century. An act of Parliament in 1534 cut it loose from Rome and marked its beginning as a state church. The adoption of the famous Thirty-nine Articles in 1571 gave it a stable theological framework. The Puritan thrust for reform from about 1560 to 1660 was repulsed. The reaction that followed saw the most devout members of the clergy ejected from their churches, and a great wave of immorality swept the country. At the outset of the eighteenth century, unbelief was the dominant religious mood, and crass immorality characterized society generally.

How Methodism Came to Be
Certainly righteousness was in eclipse because of all this, but not totally. Here and there were men and women who remained devout in spite of England's sad moral decay.

A small but important group of these could be found at Oxford University. In November, 1729, four young men of the campus, two of whom were John and Charles Wesley, began meeting together several evenings a week to read, chiefly from the Greek New Testament. The number increased until by 1735 there were approximately fourteen.

These men were all zealous members of the Church of England. Their stated objective was to be "downright Bible Christians." They were orderly in the conduct of their lives and regular in the taking of the Sacrament of Communion. A young gentleman of the University observed this and remarked, "Here is a new set of Methodists sprung up." He was reviving a name that had been given some ancient physicians of Rome, applying it now in derision. But the name stuck, and soon this group was known all over the university as "Methodists."

John Wesley

John Wesley quickly became the recognized leader of the company, and for this reason, we will take a closer look at his life.

His father, Samuel, was a humble clergyman of the Church of England. His mother, Susanna, was one of the most unusual women of the age and a descendant of Puritan stock. Wesley himself was ordained a priest of the Church of England in 1725 and, at the age of twenty-three, became Greek lecturer in Lincoln College, Oxford University.

The John Wesley of 1729 took his religion seriously, a fact which is not surprising when one considers the piety and strength of character of his mother. He could scarcely have been more ardent in study, devotion, and good works. He was prompted to these not only by his mother's influence but also by his notion at the time that it was a man's duty to keep the divine law perfectly in order to be justified before God. He knew that holy character was to be every Christian's goal. Even so, his heart was not at rest through this strenuous period.

In 1735, he set sail for the young colony of Georgia where he planned to be a missionary to the Indians. His voyage threw him into the company of a group of twenty-six German Christians, called Moravians. They were a pious lot, but this was not what most caught his attention. When a bad storm arose during the crossing, the Moravians continued to sing and worship. Wesley, by contrast, was frightened. He saw that in spite of all his religion he was afraid to die.

His term in Georgia was arduous but disquieting. As a result, two years later he closed his Georgia journal with the words:

> It is now two years and almost four months since I left my native country in order to teach the Georgian Indians the nature of Christianity. But what have I learned myself in the meantime? Why (what I least of all suspected), that I, who went to America to convert others, was never myself converted to God.

Back in London, Wesley met a Moravian named Peter Bohler. They talked together often, and in their talks Bohler was able to show Wesley the reason for his spiritual dissatisfaction. He taught him the way of salvation by faith. What Bohler said of the nature of saving faith was precisely what the Church of England held in its official statement, that it is "a sure trust and confidence which a man hath in God, that through the merits of Christ his sins are forgiven, and he is reconciled to the favor of God."

On May 24, 1738, Wesley's long search was rewarded. Following the way of faith as outlined by Bohler, he had an evangelical conversion which marked the beginning of a new era both for him and for his beloved England. Of this conversion we will say more later.

Not many months passed before Wesley was preaching to growing numbers that man is saved not by the number of his good works but by personal faith in Christ. At the same time his friend, George Whitefield, a powerful orator, was preaching the same message to expanding audiences. And his brother Charles, who, only days before John, had come to his own evangelical conversion, was the third member of the trio. England was now to hear from these three men.

By 1739, a spiritual awakening had begun. At the center of it was the Anglican clergyman John Wesley. For the remainder of his long ministry he preached, taught, and wrote with unusual ardor and effectiveness. The results of his earnest labors, supplemented by the faithful services of growing numbers of converts, are amazing to ponder.

The Methodist Revival

By the end of John Wesley's life, in 1791, the movement called Methodism had made itself felt in England, Ireland, Scotland, and Wales. It had also become a powerful force in the religious life of the new nation in America. There were more than one hundred thirty thousand Methodists in England and America and close to a million adherents. England had been saved from a bloodletting revolution such as swept France in the late eighteenth century. A new spiritual vitality had come to the established church, and the nation had a revived conscience on matters of right and wrong.

It is impossible to trace in detail all the factors that made this the greatest revival of religion since the first century. But let us look at three of the most important features of this religious awakening of the eighteenth century.

1. *An Emphasis on Nurture*

In 1738, the year in which they experienced evangelical conversions, both John and Charles Wesley were invited to preach in various parts of London. This they did, with a twofold objective: to show what true Christianity was and to convince their hearers to embrace it.

Charles and John created a stir. Some people bitterly opposed what they heard. Others were awakened spiritually, responding to the good news. Those who responded began to experience persecution. They turned to the Wesleys who advised them to meet as often as possible to pray, to read the Scriptures, and to encourage one another. But this was not enough. They wanted John Wesley to talk to them and instruct them. He visited them for this purpose but soon found that the rapidly increasing number of converts made his visits increasingly difficult.

He then advised them to meet together on Thursday nights for prayer and instruction. The groups thus formed became the first Methodist societies. The procedure they adopted was so successful in conserving and instructing new Christians that it became a basic part of the Methodist revival. In the words of Mr. Wesley, these gatherings were held by the converts "in order to pray together, to receive the word of exhortation, and to watch over one another in love, that they might help each other to work out their salvation."

Later, Wesley observed that the majority of those who were awakened and who began to "fear God and work righteousness," but who did not become a part of a nurture group, soon "grew faint in their minds and fell back into what they were before." The value of the societies as a means of Christian encouragement and growth can scarcely be overestimated. In fact, their thoroughness in promoting the nurture of the spiritual life contributed greatly to the success of eighteenth-century Methodism.

2. *An Emphasis on Lay Participation*

John Wesley, the undisputed leader in the eighteenth century evangelical awakening, showed remarkable skill in organizing the fruit of revival for permanency. But it must not be inferred that human agency in this or in any other aspect of the revival can account for its sweep. The eighteenth century saw what one called "a rich outpouring of the living Spirit of God on the nation." The Spirit of God was the real director of this marvelous movement.

Nonetheless, the Holy Spirit used men. He used the Wesleys and George Whitefield. And He used the converts of the revival. Laymen were used in some cases by the wisdom of the leaders, but in other cases the Holy Spirit had to overrule long-standing prejudices to give unordained men their rightful place in the movement.

As the revival spread, the growth in members made it more difficult for the few leaders to be sure that their new members were walking in the paths of righteousness. Converts, it must be remembered, were coming from the near-pagan elements in the populace, and relapses were not uncommon.

The class meeting arose out of this problem. The society at Bristol was seeking a satisfactory way to meet its debt on a new chapel. A group was discussing the matter when one suggested that each member give a penny a week toward this end. When told that some could not afford even this, he volunteered: "Then put eleven of the poorest with me; and if they can give anything, well: I will call on them weekly; and if they can give nothing, I will give for them as well as for myself." He followed to suggest that each of the others likewise take charge of eleven with the same thought in mind.

Thus began the class meeting, an important feature of the revival. Wesley soon observed that this not only met the problem of the debt but also the need for the personal supervision of converts. Through the class meeting, membership in the societies was kept largely to those who were in earnest to "flee from the wrath to come." Class leaders learned how to "reprove, rebuke, exhort with all long-suffering and doctrine" (2 Timothy 4:2, KJV). Of no less importance, the organization of the classes involved the development of lay leadership to fill the positions of class leaders at the approximate ratio of one to twelve.

Lay participation characterized the revival in its other aspects as well. When the weight of temporal affairs became heavy, Wesley chose prudent men to handle accounts and send relief to the poor. These were called stewards. (They met together at six o'clock on Thursday mornings.) Again, in this way laymen were used as partners in the revival, and they discharged their tasks with growing skill and wisdom.

Soon the work of visiting the sick grew beyond the stewards' resources. The matter was laid before the society. Volunteers were requested. From the volunteers, Wesley chose forty-six and set them systematically to their task. They were called Visitors of the Sick, and their work, Wesley observed, resembled that done by the deacons of the early church.

Besides all this, lay preachers were raised up by the Holy Spirit to enlarge the work of the revival. Wesley had favored the use of laymen in such activities as handling finances and visiting the sick. But he was a staunch churchman, and opposed letting unordained men preach. Notwithstanding his prejudices at this point, he was compelled to recognize the hand of God on one and then another of these men who were preaching by a divine compulsion. Thus, lay preachers were also used in the spread of revival.

The large place filled by laymen in the evangelical awakening must be recognized. They shared through the societies in the building up of one another in love. They gave spiritual leadership in class meetings. They were involved in temporal service as stewards and in spiritual ministration as Visitors of the Sick. And, under the supervision of the Spirit, many were set apart to preach the gospel, which they did with amazing effectiveness.

3. *Field Preaching*

The Methodist emphases on Christian nurture and lay activity in themselves cannot account for the one hundred thirty thousand Methodists and nearly one million adherents at the time of John Wesley's death. To account for such phenomenal growth we must consider the practice of field preaching which developed during the revival.

John Wesley, again because of his ecclesiastical background, could not easily reconcile himself to the practice of preaching in the fields after the fashion of George Whitefield. To him this seemed gross. However, Wesley's preaching caused more of a spiritual awakening than the established church could tolerate, and as a result, one church after another closed its doors to him. Soon he was shut out from the pulpit of every church in and around London.

But he dared not be silent. After a short struggle he laid aside his scruples against preaching outside of established churches and preached wherever he could get a hearing, first in the middle of Moorfields. His testimony of this occasion was: "Here were thousands upon thousands, abundantly more than any church could contain; and numbers among them who never went to any church or place of public worship at all."

The closing of the churches to Wesley actually proved to be a providence. On one occasion, as many as thirty thousand heard him preach in the open air. Thousands were convicted of sin and converted to God. So effective did field preaching prove, in fact, that Wesley himself in later years observed that should field preaching cease, the revival itself would wane.

It is safe to say that Methodism in England was originally characterized by at least three distinctive features: It was marked first by an evangelistic passion that took the gospel to the masses wherever they could be found; secondly, by an emphasis on

Christian nurture that produced saints by the thousands; and finally, by a development and use of Christian laymen in such numbers that the awakening was multiplied a thousandfold.

When Methodism Came to America

Such evangelical fervor would quite naturally soon make itself felt in the New World. Almost from the start, the young colonies felt the shock waves of what was happening in England. We turn now to a brief survey of how the Methodist movement fared in America.

Many names are associated with the beginnings of Methodism in the young America. George Whitefield preached in the colonies as early as 1738 and intermittently thereafter for many years. But his converts were not organized into societies. They were left to the care of existing churches.

Barbara Heck has been called the mother of Methodism in the New World, and her influence on her cousin, Philip Embury, has been cited as her greatest contribution to the movement. Embury had been a local preacher in Ireland, but in the New World he was overcome by discouragement. Barbara Heck's persistent urgings were responsible for his return to his calling, and soon he was holding services in his own home in New York.

Though many other names could be cited, Thomas Coke and Francis Asbury played the most significant roles in the beginnings of American Methodism. Dr. Coke was a learned man. Francis Asbury was an itinerant preacher sent out from England.

In the last quarter of the eighteenth century, the War of Independence disrupted church life in America. At its conclusion, the Church of England no longer existed as such in the infant nation, and the Protestant Episcopal Church was not yet organized. Since Methodists had continued to look to the Church of England for the Sacrament of Communion, a great need arose for ordained men.

Wesley urged the Bishop of London to ordain one man who could meet this need in America. The bishop refused. Wesley thereupon again laid aside his scruples and ordained Dr. Coke as a superintendent, with Francis Asbury to serve with him.

The Methodist Episcopal Church came into being at the

famous Christmas Conference of 1784. Its statement of faith was twenty-five articles of religion which Wesley himself had prepared by revising and abbreviating the historic Thirty-Nine Articles of the Church of England.

The young church flourished on the frontier of the world. Circuit riders and camp meetings served to broadcast its message and to enlarge its numbers. It soon became a great force in society. Prominent people came to be numbered among its members, and the stigma which being a Methodist had once cast began to vanish.

Unfortunately, spiritual decline set in. By the middle of the nineteenth century, all was not well in the Methodist Episcopal Church. Problems had arisen which we will outline presently. In what was known as the Genesee Conference in New York State, a sharp cleavage developed between two kinds of Methodist preachers. This cleavage, which deepened across many years, resulted finally in the organization of the Free Methodist Church in Pekin, New York, on August 23, 1860. To understand the nature of the division and the necessity for the new church, we will now consider the issues one at a time.

1. *Doctrine*

According to the Wesleys, believers are sanctified wholly, not by the coming of death nor by the accumulation of good works, but by an act of faith in the redeeming God. So focal was this message that it had been called "the distinctive doctrine of Methodism."

There were men in the Genesee Conference who continued to proclaim it. But others opposed it, claiming that one is entirely sanctified at the moment he is justified, and nothing more is to be expected but growth. This, it is well known, was a point of view Wesley himself had strenuously opposed as unscriptural. The two views were at issue in the conflict which made the Free Methodist Church a necessity.

2. *Secret Societies*

The unfortunate struggle was sharpened by the fact that about thirty clergymen of the conference held membership in secret societies. This was no mere side issue. One firsthand witness stated that the conflict actually had its origin "in the connection of several of the more prominent preachers (of the conference) with the Odd Fellows and Masons."

These men decided beforehand, in secret gatherings, how they would vote in conference business. They used their influence to intimidate younger members of the conference either to keep silent or to vote with them. They even threatened that if two presiding elders of the other side were not removed, the bishop would find himself without thirty men to take appointments. The two elders were removed. By their tactics they won for themselves the name, "The Regency Party," *rulers of sorts*. In turn, they gave those who were contending for Methodist doctrine and practice the name, "Nazirites," taken from a rigorous Old Testament sect.

3. *Slavery*

Wesley had looked with disfavor upon the practice of holding slaves, contending that the practice was utterly inconsistent with Christianity. Through the influence of the Methodist revival in England, slavery in that country had been abolished without the firing of a shot.

The Methodist Episcopal Church in the New World had begun with the same bold conviction. But very early in its history its position had been modified. By the middle of the nineteenth century the new church was no longer clear in its stand. On the very eve of the Civil War, in fact, thousands of its members held slaves.

This too was an issue in the struggle that made the Free Methodist Church necessary. Those who had been derisively called Nazirites held clear and uncompromising Methodist convictions on the dignity of all human life. Their stand served only to sharpen the growing antagonism of the Regency Party.

In 1864, the end of the Civil War marked the blood purchase of freedom for the slaves of the American states. But the founders of the Free Methodist Church had shown themselves to be ahead of their times in their social conscience, having stood for such freedom on Christian grounds long before the war began.

4. *Rented Pews*

Wesley, it will be remembered, preached in the fields so that all might hear the gospel. His meetinghouses had been plain and simple for the same reason. He had even been attacked by the elite of his day as a social leveler. But by the middle of the nineteenth century, the practice of renting pews had become quite general in America, particularly in the Genesee Conference of the Methodist Episcopal Church.

In the eyes of those who maintained loyalty to the principles of historic Methodism, such a practice was a serious offense. It tended to recognize unduly the wealthy in society and to discriminate against the poor. Those who were too poor to pay for a pew were likely to be too proud to advertise the fact by sitting in a specially designated section of the church. Thus, the practice of renting pews appeared to violate the Methodist principle that the gospel is to be preached freely to all men. This, too, was an issue in the conflict of the late 1850s.

5. *Worldliness*

The England to which the Methodist revival came was almost completely dominated by the world-spirit. It was a society largely alienated from God and under the sway of Satan. This fact reflected itself in the amusements, the recreation, the literature, and even the religion of the time. In all of these, to some degree, the worship of self had replaced the worship of God with the result that the lust of the flesh, the lust of the eye, and the pride of life unashamedly dominated the minds and hearts of the English people.

A striking feature of Methodism in this era was its frank renunciation of the world-spirit. In contrast to the worship of self which reflected itself generally in the society of the early eighteenth century, the Methodists had set glorifying God in all things as their supreme object. They were in the world, a fact clearly evident in their influence on the culture of their century, but they were definitely not of the world. Their uncompromising stand at this point made them a great influence for righteousness, but it subjected them to much persecution.

Unfortunately, the Genesee Conference of the Methodist Episcopal Church, in the middle of the nineteenth century, was not characterized by such a sense of separation from the world. To the contrary, worldliness was becoming a growing menace to the fulfillment of the Methodist mission. For only one example,

Christian devotion waned, and with it Christian giving declined. To solve the problem of reduced support, some churches began to sponsor clambakes and chowder feeds to raise sorely needed funds. These activities were soon followed by card parties, dances, and drinking parties. One prominent city church even made one of the largest liquor dealers in its city a trustee and church treasurer.

In contrast, those who had been cast in the role of reformers in the Genesee Conference held out for the spiritual and physical enlargement of the church by spiritual means. They preached clearly the cardinal doctrines of Methodism. They insisted in their preaching that those who were "alive unto God" would show that fact in all areas of their lives.

The churches they served experienced revivals, and membership grew steadily. Being men of great effectiveness they were Methodists in the historic sense of the word--spiritually concerned, evangelistically motivated, and restless for the enlargement of the kingdom of God on earth.

The Organization of the Free Methodist Church

The cleavage was clear. It can be traced across many years in the Genesee Conference of the Methodist Episcopal Church. The seed of the conflict had been sown long before the middle of the century. It was in the year 1857, however, that the division came to an issue brought about inadvertently by the pen of a conference minister, the Reverend Benjamin Titus Roberts.

B. T. Roberts was a young man of piety, conviction, and learning. His first formal training was for the practice of law. But a profound conversion in his youth turned him toward the ministry, and he attended Wesleyan University, Middletown, Connecticut. He proved his ability by teaching school and at the same time carrying on his university work several terms without benefit of instructors. He received honors as one of the top students of his class.

His piety showed in the work he did as a young minister. His object was always to promote revivals of religion, and such revivals caused his work to prosper in the churches he served. At his first church, the membership increased the first year by forty.

He also saw the church building improved and a long-standing debt on the parsonage paid off.

Roberts's ability to think clearly on moral issues was evident in his university days. Even then, his well-awakened Methodist conscience saw the evils of slavery and racial discrimination. Later, as a minister in the city of Buffalo, New York, he was grieved at the practical effects of the rental of pews. He saw that this favored the wealthy and led to the neglect of the poor. Again his Methodist conscience was offended.

He used his gifted pen in an effort to stimulate concern for reform in the church he dearly loved. In 1857 he produced an article for publication entitled "New School Methodism" which brought out the essential difference between the two points of view that existed in the conference. In doing so, it brought clearly to light that those who held positions of leadership in the conference, members of the Regency Party, had really departed from essential Methodist doctrines and principles.

His carefully reasoned article showed that they no longer held to Methodist teaching on sanctification. Nor were they committed to heartfelt religion and a life marked by simplicity and godliness. They had veered from Methodism in renting pews and refusing to face the issue of worldliness within the church.

The publication of the article gave the Regency Party occasion to stimulate real crisis in the conference. Roberts was charged at the annual conference and committed to trial. He was convicted and reproved by the bishop. What charge could be leveled for the publication of an article which no one was willing to refute? Nothing less than "immoral and unchristian conduct." Then, at the same annual meeting, he was appointed to serve a church at Pekin, New York, to which he went without complaint. Here again his work prospered.

But the fracture was beyond healing. A second charge was brought against him when a layman, without Roberts's permission, republished "New School Methodism." In succeeding months, other ministers were likewise brought under attack by the Regency Party. Furthermore, the names of laymen who were sympathetic with the men supporting historic Methodism were arbitrarily removed from the church rolls by the hundreds.

Roberts was expelled from the Methodist Episcopal Church along with another clergyman. The account of their trials and the report of firsthand witnesses show that injustice was done. Besides, hundreds of sympathetic laymen were deprived of their membership for no reason except that they were in sympathy with an effort to keep the doctrines and practices of historic Methodism alive. What was to be done?

Roberts appealed his case to the General Conference to convene in May, 1860. The laymen endeavored to meet in "bands" while they awaited the action of the General Conference. Twice in the intervening two years, laymen's conventions were held. At these conventions, protest was made against the high-handed methods of the Regency Party, but a resolution was also passed in which these laymen declared their devotion to their church and their unwillingness to secede. They were committed Methodists, and they intended to remain so as long as possible.

However, in violation of legal rights and Christian courtesy, B. T. Roberts's appeal was denied in May of 1860. The laymen who had been deprived of their membership, as well as Roberts and several other expelled ministers who shared his convictions, had only two courses before them.

They wanted to remain in the Methodist Episcopal Church and promote revival and evangelism through the preaching of the Wesleyan message. They had repeatedly stated so, but this course had been closed to them by the actions of the General Conference of 1860. As an unlikely alternative, they could be spiritual nomads, destitute of any church home or church fellowship.

But they were too deeply committed to Methodist principles of fellowship to take this course. Wesley, remember, had organized new Christians into societies so they could be nurtured and built up in the faith. Laymen, who had been expelled from local congregations in the two years prior to 1860, had been urged to follow the same course of action, awaiting their reinstatement by the General Conferences. Converts won during that two-year period had also been made members of bands or societies. They needed a church home.

Following General Conference, only one course was open to

them. They did not move hastily, but on August 23, 1860, a group of eighty laymen and fifteen ministers met in conference at Pekin, New York. There, in a camp meeting grove on the farm of I. M. Chesbrough, they organized a new denomination.

This infant church was to be in the train of historic Methodism as we shall subsequently see. It was named the Free Methodist Church because the adjective "free" reflected the issues in its origin. It was to be marked by freedom from slavery, freedom from secret societies, free seats in all churches, and the freedom of the Spirit in worship. Benjamin Titus Roberts was elected to be the first general superintendent.

Four Things to Remember

It's hard to realize the vast changes of the last one hundred twenty-five years.

When our branch of the Christian church came into being, for example, there were no automobiles, airplanes, radios, televisions, synthetic fabrics, paperbacks, or air conditioners. Now, these products of genius and technology touch every area of our lives, practically shaping our culture.

This vast technological change can make the events of a century and a quarter ago seem irrelevant to the present. In fact, it can make anything but the present seem remote and unimportant. Therefore, there are some things we must charge ourselves to remember as we close this chapter.

1. *Principles Never Change*

It's true that the issues that exercised the consciences of B. T. Roberts and kindred spirits in the late 1850s are not issues that concern us today. For example, slavery, so controversial back then, does not exist now in North America.

What was at root in those issues, however, is as timeless as the gospel itself. Our forefathers opposed slavery because they believed in the sanctity before God of all human life. They believed this in turn gave all human life a dignity before man.

The sanctity of all human life is a foremost issue of our day, though not in the same modes as during the last century. Consider some of the many problems of our times that reflect this issue: racial discrimination, abortion as a means of birth control, wife and child abuse, and both physical and emotional violence.

In these matters, Free Methodists should stand for principles that never change--the issues of righteousness. "The incurable sickness of the world," writes John Bright, "is due, more than to any economic cause, to the total and corporate failure of man in the realm of righteousness" (*The Kingdom of God*, Abingdon Press: 1953, p. 93. Used by permission).

2. *The Most Basic Issue of All*

At the same time, so far as the church is concerned, one issue stands ahead of all others--the gospel. Consider the focus of the New Testament. It begins with four separate accounts of the coming of Jesus Christ, highlighting important features of his life, death, and resurrection. After the four gospels, each succeeding book bears on the gospel in some particular way. It was the proclamation of this gospel, authenticated by the power of God's Spirit, that brought the church into being across the Roman world. It is the same gospel which sustains and energizes the church to the present.

Whenever this gospel ceases to be the force at the center of all a church is and does, even if that church continues to stand for certain principles, that stand is likely at best to be sectarian. If, on the other hand, the gospel is talked of glowingly, but not applied in such a way as to make that church a moral force in its world, the church will be little more than one more social organization in society.

The central issue of righteousness is one's personal acceptance before God. To this, the gospel speaks with force. A church is a community of men, women, youth, and children who have been accounted righteous before God through faith in the saving death of His Son, Jesus Christ. They belong to one another because they belong to Him. But such a community can scarcely be indifferent to the issues of righteousness in its world.

When we think of the history of our church, at the same time we must think of the gospel. Only the gospel can give a Christian perspective to the moral issues of any particular period of time.

3. *The Roots of the Free Methodist Church*

The history of any true branch of the church of Jesus Christ must trace its roots to the people of the Bible. Neither the eighteenth-century evangelical revival nor the sixteenth-century Reformation take us back far enough. The Free Methodist Church has surface roots in these periods, but its deep roots go back to Abraham, Isaac, and Jacob.

The Bible is very clear that God has always had a people. They are an elect people, called by God to live in obedience to Him, formed by covenant and declared to be a witnessing community to the whole world. Their history is checkered and their responses to God's call have not always been laudable. Nevertheless God has loved them, visiting them in judgment in their times of rebellion, calling them back to obedience, and through them giving the world His Son, Jesus Christ.

The church of the New Testament is continuous with the church of the Old Testament. In the New Testament as much as in the Old, Abraham is the father of the faithful. The New Testament completes the Old in reporting the fulfillment of all God's promises in Jesus Christ. But in both Testaments, the best synonym for the church is the people of God.

The Free Methodist Church has been fashioned somewhat by geography, somewhat by sociology, and somewhat by periodic issues and accidents of history. The same is true of every Christian body. But we insist that behind all these shaping influences, we want an identity with the people of God of all ages who trace their roots to the prophets and apostles of the Scriptures.

4. *Alive to God Today*

If we wish to understand our present, we must understand our past. Nevertheless, even this worthy exercise has its perils. It is a short step from studying our past to trusting our past to sustain us. This makes us traditionalists, and traditionalism is attended by inflexibility and irrelevance.

Our history does indeed supply us with valuable insights, and we carry into the present certain of its timeless values. But we are not saved by our past. The Savior of the church is Jesus Christ who is "the same yesterday, today, and forever."

The church at its best is marked by a present lively trust in God, through Jesus Christ its living Lord. It is marked by a submission to His will and an obedience to His commands. The electricity that floods a building with light is not electricity generated in a previous century. It is today's electricity for today's needs. So, the life that energizes the church is the life of the living God, mediated today through God's Holy Spirit.

Protestantism is "constant renewal at the hand of God," writes Robert McAfee Brown. As you enter into the joys and responsibilities of belonging to the Free Methodist Church, help to make that true for your church too.

For Review:
1.   What major events brought the Church of England to the condition in which it was found at the beginning of the eighteenth century?

2.   List three features of the Methodist revival of the eight-eenth century that accounted for its spread and strength.

3.   What issues were involved in the conflict of the nineteenth century that made the Free Methodist Church necessary?

4.   What steps were taken by B. T. Roberts and his associates to assist their remaining in the Methodist Episcopal Church?

5.   Indicate the place, date, and circumstances under which the Free Methodist Church was organized.

For Further Reading:
Marston, L. R. "Benjamin Titus Roberts: Founder of Free Methodism" (filmstrip with script). Winona Lake, Indiana: Light and Life Press, 1973. (Light and Life Press is now located in Indianapolis, Indiana.)

Marston, L. R. *From Age to Age a Living Witness*. Winona Lake, Indiana: Light and Life Press, 1960. (A concise church history text or encyclopedia. Articles may also be used for general background material.) (Light and Life Press is now located in Indianapolis, Indiana.)

For Further Thought:
What features of the original Methodist movement as set forth in this chapter could profitably be renewed in the life of our church?

People affect history. Who were the ten most influential histori-cal people in Free Methodism?

CHAPTER SIX

Thousands outside and inside the church are beginning to see: We are created to live under orders. In this way lies true freedom. We need to put our lives under the direction of someone else.

For the Christian disciple, that someone else is Jesus Christ. His call to discipleship is recorded in the Scriptures (Matthew 16:24; Mark 8:34, Luke 9:23). The implications of this call were worked out by the early church and these are recorded in the apostolic letters to the churches. Our own development as Christian disciples is linked to careful study of and obedient response to the Scriptures.

The Meaning of Discipleship

Our son worked in a newspaper office next to the desk of Donna, a young, charming, and thoroughly modern miss. Donna was an avowed secularist. Believing solely in the here and now, she accepted no absolute reference points outside herself and acknowledged no obligations not self-imposed. She gave the air of being free, untrammeled, open.

In one of their wide-ranging noon-hour discussions, our son described what radical Christian discipleship would entail. Donna listened raptly, her countenance responding affirmatively to the description. At the end she said, "Hey, that's neat."

In one way or another she had often expressed her need to live autonomously. On this occasion, the need gave place to a deeper one--the need to live under orders.

Donna may have caught her first glimpse of what thousands outside and inside the church are beginning to see: We are created to live under orders. In this way lies true freedom. We need to put our lives under the direction of someone else.

For the Christian disciple, that someone else is Jesus Christ. His call to discipleship is recorded in the Scriptures (Matthew 16:24; Mark 8:34; Luke 9:23). The implications of this call were worked out by the early church and these are recorded in the apostolic letters to the churches. Our own development as Christian disciples is linked to careful study of and obedient response to the Scriptures.

Some say the church as it exists today cannot promote discipleship because of its own defects--its bondage to culture, its lack of a face-to-face life of fellowship, its casualness about eternal matters. Others counter this, calling attention to the desire for spiritual renewal arising within the institution and the pockets of renewal already forming in many places.

As we explore another dimension of belonging, let us pursue the recovery of discipleship within the life of the church. In this chapter, we'll look at three aspects of Christian discipleship.

Living in Obedience to Christ

We can understand discipleship as living in obedience to

Jesus Christ when we think of the original twelve disciples. Jesus was with them physically. He talked to them--teaching, commending, reproving. They traveled together and they went to Him with their questions. In Jesus, the Twelve had a master to mediate their arguments and pass judgment on their opinions.

We moderns are far removed from the scene of His travels. Life is different for us. Jesus Christ is no longer present in the flesh. How then can we hope to live in discipleship to Him?

There are certain Christian affirmations in the New Testament that answer this question. After Jesus was crucified He rose from death to become living Lord over His people. "Lo, I am with you always, even to the end of the age," He told His disciples when He gave them the Great Commission (Matthew 28:19-20, NASB). He had mysteriously promised them, "I will not leave you desolate; I will come to you" (John 14:18, RSV). He was speaking of His own Spirit, the Holy Spirit, who makes Jesus real to all His followers.

Paul, the Apostle, never saw Jesus during His earthly ministry, yet the risen Savior addressed him on the Damascus road and called him to discipleship. From that time on, Paul lived out a whole ministry seeking to carry out the task assigned him. Many years later, in a final farewell to the Ephesian elders at the seaport city of Miletus, he said, "But life to me is not a thing to waste words on, provided that when I finish my race, I have carried out the mission the Lord Jesus gave me--and that was to bear witness to the Good News of God's grace" (Acts 20:24, *Jerusalem Bible*).

If one man could live out his life in obedience to Jesus Christ a generation after His earthly life, why can't great numbers do it twenty centuries later? The same Holy Spirit who made Jesus real to Paul makes Him contemporary to us.

Commitment to Personal Integrity

After the Resurrection, the first generation of Christians came to be characterized as people of "the Way" (Acts 24:14, 22). Defending himself before Felix, the governor, Paul gave a thumbnail sketch of the sect which had won for itself the name Christian: (1) they worshiped the God of Israel; (2) they believed the writings of the Old Testament; (3) they believed in a coming resurrection of both the just and the unjust; (4) because of these convictions, they were compelled to live lives marked by integrity before God and man.

Something similar happened eighteen centuries later when the Methodist Revival spread throughout the British Isles and leaped across the ocean. Methodists took on characteristics that marked them as people of "the Way." They worshiped the living God, took the Christian Scriptures seriously, came to be filled with hope of a life to come, and, as a result, became marked by qualities of personal integrity in this life.

In 1739, people in and around London began to ask John and Charles Wesley for spiritual guidance in their quest for true righteousness. At first this guidance was given to individuals and later to a society that met on Thursday evenings. As the revival spread, additional societies were formed in other places, and membership grew rapidly.

But growth introduced problems. Many converts showed they had received the Word into hearts that offered resistance, like the rocky hearts Jesus described in His parable (Matthew 13). They responded with vigor, but when persecution came they withered, returning to their old ways. Furthermore, within the societies, problems of discipline arose. These problems threatened to destroy the spiritual power of the young Methodist movement by filling its membership with a mixed multitude. Many were devout, but some became indifferent, and not a few reverted completely.

The General Rules

To solve this problem, John and Charles Wesley drew up a set of regulations in 1743, outlining the requirements for membership in Methodist societies. Called the "General Rules," they brought into focus the fact that the faith of all Methodists was expected to express itself in transformed living. Enforcement of these rules on many occasions reduced the size of the societies, but members were removed only after all else had failed. Enforcement proved to be in the best interests of both the societies and the unfaithful members.

More than a century later, in 1860, the founding fathers of the newly organized Free Methodist Church kept these rules as a part of its constitution. In doing so, they were recognizing the permanent value of the General Rules as guidelines for earnest Christians. At the same time, they were declaring their allegiance to historic Methodism.

Membership Covenant

In 1974, the General Conference adopted a Membership Covenant. This document put the General Rules into a new form for public use while at the same time preserving the essence of the historic statement.

It must be stressed that the purpose of the membership covenant is not to deprive a Christian of his liberty in Christ. Nor is it to shift his focus from Christ to a system of exhortations and prohibitions. The purpose is to offer guidance and counsel to the Christian who wishes to commit himself to a style of life consistent with Christian discipleship.

Based on the historic General Rules of Methodism, here is the membership covenant and explanatory comments.

I confess Jesus Christ as my personal Savior and Lord and will continue to walk with him by faith. I commit myself to know God in His full sanctifying grace.

A Christian does not stop with the confession of his sins. He confesses Jesus Christ as His Savior too. The Apostle Paul wrote, "If you confess with your lips that Jesus is Lord and believe in your heart that God raised him from the dead, you will be saved" (Romans 10:9, RSV). Here is the starting place for mature church membership.

Jesus Christ died for our salvation, rose from death, and is now Lord of His people. The focus of our membership commitment is to acknowledge these realities and to live out our lives by faith under His sovereign leadership. Since our sanctification--separation to God and moral cleansing--begins when we confess Jesus Christ as Savior and Lord and are given His life within us, it is a part of our initial membership commitment to seek the fullest possible experience of His sanctifying grace.

As Regards God

1. I will reverence the name of God.

This is a restatement of the third of the Ten Commandments (Exodus 20:7), which forbids us to take the name of God in vain and is usually considered a prohibition of blasphemy, or swearing. But, more broadly, to take the name of God in vain means to take it lightly. We exhort other people to hold the name of God in such reverence that His name cannot be used in any trifling manner.

Humor that reflects upon the name of God and slang that is evidently a modification of the names or characteristics of deity are inappropriate in the speech of anyone who has seen God's holiness. The command of Jesus is: "But let your communication be, yea, yea; nay, nay: for whatsoever is more than these cometh of evil" (Matthew 5:37, KJV).

2. I will observe the Lord's Day in worship, Christian fellowship and service, renewal of mind and spirit, avoiding all unnecessary commerce, labors, travel, and pleasures which detract from the moral and spiritual purposes of the day.

In Jesus' day, strict religious sects had made the commandment concerning the Sabbath a great burden on the human spirit. Their prohibitions made it seem sinful even to be humane on the Sabbath. Jesus healed on the Sabbath and was censored by them for doing so.

The Old Testament Sabbath, observed on Saturday, commemorated God's completion of His creation and His subsequent rest from His labors. His people symbolized this fact by desisting from work. Hence, the Sabbath is called the day of rest. Christians observe the first day of the week, Sunday, and refer to it as the Lord's Day--the day of resurrection and beginnings.

Our problem in observing the Lord's Day is the opposite of the Pharisaic problem. Secularism has nearly obliterated, even for Christians, the special religious nature of Sunday. The Free Methodist Church wishes to help its people experience the benefits of a special Lord's Day observance without putting upon them a legalistic burden.

Sunday is a special day for public worship. Those who

reduce this feature of the day down to only an hour for worship in the morning will find themselves siding more with the secular culture than with the people of God. Their church will suffer too. A Sunday begun and ended in corporate worship gives tone to the human spirit and testimony to a secular culture.

For those so inclined, Sunday is a good day to minister to the sick, the shut-ins, and the aged, because the time is available.

Those who work in factories or offices or serve at the management level of business live stressfully all week. For their own benefit, they should guard the Lord's day from unnecessary commerce, labors, travels, and pleasures.

Jesus said, "The Sabbath was made for man, and not man for the Sabbath" (Mark 2:27). So long as man is man, he will need at least one day for special renewal of the spirit.

3. I will not engage in any form of false worship such as spiritism, witchcraft, and astrology.

The Christian faith is monotheistic, believing in one God only. It does not even worship Jesus as a separate god, but as God the Son--one person of the triune Godhead. This monotheism is reflected in the first commandment: "Thou shalt have no other gods before me."

But all through history the people of God have been beset with the temptation to worship other gods. In ancient Israel there was the lure to Baal worship. Later, Jesus warned, "You cannot serve God and mammon" (Matthew 6:24, RSV). In recent times materialism has tended to deaden the devotion of Christians. Luther said that the human heart is a perpetual forge of idols.

Our generation has seen a great rise in the worship of the occult. Great numbers have dabbled in everything from Ouija boards to devil worship. The Free Methodist Church wants its people to recognize idolatry for what it is--the worship of the creature rather than the Creator--and to take seriously the command Jesus himself endorsed: "You shall worship the Lord your God and him only shall you serve" (Matthew 4:10, RSV).

4. I will abstain from membership in secret societies and oath-bound lodges, and, recognizing that the religious nature of such organizations tends to divide the Christian's loyalty and confuse his Christian faith, I will keep myself free to follow the will of God in all things.

The argument is sometimes raised that lodges do much good through their charities and benevolent institutions. And they are represented as a harmless form of social relationship. Why then does the Free Methodist Church, one of several, forbid its members to belong?

First, secret orders require pledges of secrecy in company with other persons who may be non-Christians or even atheists. This binds the Christian conscience and compromises his loyalty to Jesus Christ. Second, secret orders are religious in nature. (You will see both these points more fully explained in the *Book of Discipline*, ¶A/321).

Once I was on the island of Okinawa, south of Japan, waiting to make a plane connection. About twenty brightly suited men, an inspiration team for a lodge on a mission to solicit members, were present. I asked one of the leaders what one had to do to join his organization. In a terse paragraph, he gave me a statement on his lodge's way to salvation. He concluded with, "It's a long hard road," making it clear that salvation is something one does for himself by hard work.

For Christians, salvation is by grace through faith.

5. I will seek to grow in the knowledge and love of God by consistent use of the means of grace such as public worship of God, the ministry of the Word, the Supper of the Lord, family and private prayer, searching the Scriptures, and fasting and abstinence.

Notice that the first section of the membership covenant, "As Regards God," centers on the worship of God. It elaborates on the name of the God we worship, the observance of a special day, and the avoidance of false worship, either through the occult or competing religious organizations. It concludes, now, with a pledge to grow in the knowledge of the one true God by consistent use of the means of grace.

This point draws strongly on the third division of the historic "General Rules of the People Called Methodists." It reflects Wesley's astute observation that if awakened individuals do not find their place in the society and attend faithfully upon the means of grace, they fall back to their former life.

In our health-conscious age, we are taught the habits of a healthy life--a wholesome diet, adequate rest, exercise. Those who take health seriously reduce these matters to a nearly unconscious regimen. In parallel manner, there are habits of holy life, reflected in the five resolutions above. Those who take the pursuit of holiness seriously, develop a regimen of life that makes a regular place for the means of grace.

As Regards Myself and All Men

1. I will show goodness and mercy to all men, and especially to the household of faith, both to their physical and spiritual needs as I have ability.

Goodness and mercy are two abstract words that stand for Christian response to human need. At the same time, they are words that describe moral attributes of God himself. Christians, therefore, are to be imitators of God in their human concerns. This part of our covenant draws on instructions the Apostle Paul gave to the Galatians: "As we have opportunity, let us do good to all men, and especially to those who are of the household of faith" (Galatians 6:10, RSV). Note, however, the comprehensiveness of the language of the covenant: We are to meet the physical and spiritual needs of others.

Methodism from the start was a religion marked by good works. One of the heresies of the time, quietism, taught that one was to do good works only if he was especially moved to do so. The Wesleys resisted this error, urging that the existence of human need was itself the summons to show goodness and mercy.

The warm heart of Methodism is reflected in this pledge. Wherever Free Methodist churches take it seriously, the sick are visited, the hungry fed, the naked clothed. Such ministries, carried out both by the corporate action of churches and by the spontaneous compassion of individual Christians, are one more witness to the world of the loyalty of the church to Jesus Christ. He said: "In as much as ye have done it unto one of the least of these my brethren, ye have done it unto me" (Matthew 25:40, KJV).

2. I will respect the rights of all persons as created in the image of God, regardless of differences of sex, race, or color.

North American society has been deeply influenced by the Judeo-Christian view of man. Basic to that view is the conviction that every human being gets his worth from the fact that he bears the image of God. That is, he is distinct from all other living creatures in the aspects of his nature that enable him to commune with God. This is the basis for human equality before God, regardless of "sex, race or color." The list could be extended to add size, intelligence, age, social standing, vocation, and so forth.

In the 1960s, social upheavals brought to light the degree to which this idealism had been eclipsed in our culture. Discrimination for reasons of race or color was brought to light and to some degree reduced by the civil rights movement. But the demeaning of humans for superficial reasons still goes on, either openly or covertly. Because such problems are culturally generated, Christians sometimes participate in them without being aware of their own prejudices.

The membership pledge to respect the rights of all calls for a show of high regard for the sanctity of human life. To work it out in practice calls for study, prayer, and discussion among Christians, guided by prophetic words from our pulpits. It will require the examination of our attitudes toward people of all classes--as to whether they are "above" or "below" the examiner --including the elderly, the unborn, the short of stature, the retarded. Christians are never free in their own spirits until they are free to respect all humans as humans.

3. I will be just in all transactions, faithful in commitments, and contract obligations with full intention to keep them.

The Christian is very much rooted in this world. Whether he is a full-fledged business person or a day laborer, he does not escape dealing in the marketplace. Transactions referred to here are exchanges of objects for money, services for money, or objects for objects. Whatever the transaction, our covenant spurs us to conduct ourselves here with the highest sense of fair play and love of neighbor.

Commitments and contract obligations are agreements made either orally or in writing. They may include a pledge to sell a bicycle or a house at an agreed price, or the promise to pay for a living room suite in an agreed-upon number of monthly payments. Whatever the agreement, we are called to integrity in fulfilling it.

There are many reasons that commend this sort of rigorous

pledge. It will help to safeguard our reputations in the community. It will restrain us from contracting unmanageable debts. The latter, in turn, will keep us free from unnecessary bondage and anxiety. But these are all secondary reasons and may be given by a good Muslim as well as a Christian. The fundamental reason for such a pledge is that Christians carry the reputation of Jesus Christ. Moreover, they are to keep themselves free to do the will of the Lord in all things.

4. I will abstain from the manufacture, sale, and use of alcoholic beverages and harmful drugs and from the cultivation, manufacture, sale, and use of tobacco.

The damage to human life stemming from the use of alcoholic beverages, harmful drugs, and tobacco has been well documented in the last half of the twentieth century. Insurance companies have published evidence that alcoholic beverages are a factor in more than half of all highway fatalities. The part they play in marriage failures, crime, illicit sex, and a score of other social problems is well known. From the medical profession we have learned the relationship between smoking tobacco and heart disease, cancer, and less-publicized complications in the pregnancies of smoking mothers.

Even so, we live in a drug-dependent culture. Consumption of alcoholic beverages goes on at an unprecedented rate, the use of tobacco (including smokeless products) continues to endanger the lives of many people, and even prescription drugs are often misused for purposes of escape. Obviously, knowledge itself does not assure a desire to refrain.

Christian faith supplies the motivation. The human body is a temple in which God's Holy Spirit takes up His dwelling (1 Corinthians 6:19). It should not be treated with contempt. We are to love God with all our minds (Matthew 22:37). One cannot do this with a mind impaired by alcohol. (It has been demonstrated that the mind's impairment begins with the first drink.)

Money is a sacred trust from God. If we spend it foolishly on personal habits that do no good and may do great harm, we will be called upon in the judgment to give an accounting of our stewardship. All these motivations come together in our loyalty to Jesus Christ. The Apostle Paul wrote: "Do not yield your members to sin as instruments of wickedness, but yield yourselves to God as men who have been brought from death to life, and your members to God as instruments of righteousness" (Romans 6:13, RSV).

5. I will abstain from all forms of gambling.

Gambling is now the world's number one growth industry. It accounts for the exchange of tens of billions of dollars yearly, and the industry shows no signs of leveling off.

With the recent rise in government-sponsored lotteries, gambling is seen as a harmless diversion even by upstanding citizens. Figures show, however, that it is expensive. For example, one study showed a total of 15 billion spent on just the lottery in the 37 states that have one (*Washington Monthly*, February 1990).

Many reasons can be given to show that gambling is inconsistent with Christian discipleship. It involves flirting with Lady Luck. It fosters immaturity in holding out to its devotees the hope of sudden wealth. It nourishes greed and avarice. Those who feel the gambling fever become superstitious in the antics they use to influence the fates. Gambling, worst of all, is habit forming and too often becomes an obsession.

"Gambling lacks both the dignity of wages earned and the honor of a gift. It takes substance from the pocket of a neighbor without yielding a fair exchange" (¶A/336.1, *Book of Discipline*).

Christians are to avoid the appearance of evil, rejoicing rather in their true freedom. "If the Son sets you free, you will be free indeed" (John 8:36).

6. I will observe the scriptural standards of simplicity, humility, modesty, propriety, purity, and good stewardship in everything I buy, use, or wear, and thereby reflect the beauty of the gospel.

This is a comprehensive call to the practice of discipleship in the realm of Christian attire. It does not describe in explicit detail what Christian dress is. To do so would lift responsibility from the individual Christian conscience and lay the groundwork for moralistic and judgmental attitudes. But it does set forth some key words around which Christian conscience can rally its insights.

Simplicity, whether in architecture or dress, calls for removal of excess adornment. It is the opposite of complexity and, with regard to attire, should stand as a caution against pretentiousness. One may dress simply and still dress in good taste, however. The Christian dresses neither to glorify nor despise the body but to reflect its dignity as God's special creation.

"*Humility*," one man observed, "is just good manners in the presence of God." From a human point of view it is unself-conscious. If we dress to advertise our humility, that is, we are demonstrating the opposite--human pride. Happy is the Christian who dresses for any occasion so that he can forget his own appearance and turn his interest toward others.

Modesty in one's attire calls for a lack of display. In its tertiary meaning, the word suggests observing the proprieties of sex, or dressing decently or chastely. Every age has a God-given sense of modesty which the Christian must not offend in his attire.

The matter of propriety in attire has been severely challenged in the last half of the twentieth century. We have been inclined to dress more according to personal whim than according to social standards. However, it must be evident upon reflection that what is appropriate at a swimming pool would not be appropriate at a church wedding or what is suitable for cleaning the attic is not suitable at the supermarket.

Purity as used in this pledge refers to moral purity. One must not dress in such a way as to offend one's own moral sense or to excite the baser impulses in another.

The practice of good stewardship in maintaining a wardrobe is particularly challenging. Affluence makes more money available to many of us, while industry and technology make available more clothes. In such circumstances, we can easily become wasteful. A wisely chosen wardrobe can bring honor to Christ and His gospel.

As Regards the Institutions of God

1. I will respect duly constituted authority in the home, church, and state, except when it is in violation of the clear teachings of the Scripture.

The structures of human life have been under widespread attack in the latter half of the twentieth century. Parents and children alike have tended to repudiate the authority of the parent in the home. The results are dire--alienation within the family, broken homes, runaway children. They are significant manifestations of a serious breakdown of authority in twentieth century life.

The renunciation of the authority of the state has also been widespread. Terrorism in the air and on the ground shows this in extreme form. But great numbers of outwardly respectable people have renounced the authority of the state by psychological withdrawal from responsibility to its structures.

The church has not escaped all this. The same antiauthority feelings manifest themselves in disregard for its stated positions regarding both doctrine and ethics. At the lower level, small excuses are often taken to disregard the leadership of pastors and the programs of congregations.

It is difficult for us to see these trends, since we are so much a part of our age that even its sicknesses may seem normal. Moreover, built right into the mentality of our culture are suspicions of authority that lead often to rebellion.

The Free Methodist Church holds before its people this ideal: Duly constituted authority is to be respected. Children are to be taught to be law-abiding as a Christian duty. The one exception to this has to do with situations where the structures of human life would call us to act contrary to the laws of God as clearly set down in Scriptures.

2. I will observe the teachings of the Scripture regarding the sanctity of the home and marriage and the nurture of children in the Christian faith.

In Genesis 1 we are taught that the most profound differentiation of our race is its differentiation into two sexes: "Male and female created he them." This differentiation is more fundamental in our existence as humans than our color or race or stature or intellectual level. We are taught in Genesis 2 that the sexes need each other and that God himself provided the institution of marriage to deal with each human's sense of incompleteness when alone. Because persons and the institution of marriage both originated in God, we refer to them as having sanctity. Therefore, we believe all Christians have a threefold responsibility: (1) to seek guidance from the Scriptures regarding the sanctity of the home and marriages; (2) to hallow the institution of marriage and the home; and, (3) to feel a sense of duty to the children of Christian homes, endeavoring to nurture them with diligence. Moses' words to Israel are instructive (Deuteronomy 6:6-9).

Nothing in this section of the membership covenant, however, should be interpreted to give the single life an inferior status. For several centuries the medieval church gave the impression that the single life was the life of higher sanctity. In our century, the rank and file in the church have absorbed the opposite idea, that unmarried adults have second-class status. In truth, God's vocation for some is the single life. At the same time, both single and married must honor the institution of marriage. Contemporary attitudes of scorn toward marriage must not be countenanced in the church.

3. I will be guided by the teachings of Scripture regarding separation, divorce, and remarriage as understood by the church, especially recognizing monogamy as God's plan for marriage.

The taking of such a pledge to commitment benefits both the church and society. Unfortunately, too often in today's society the centrality of commitment in marriage is replaced by the centrality of romance. Emphasis on romance results in marriages that disintegrate for frivolous reasons. On the other hand, the unconditional commitment of a strong Christian marriage provides a proper base for true and enduring love.

In a section on Marriage, Divorce, and Remarriage (¶A/341), our *Book of Discipline* reads: "At creation God instituted marriage for the well-being of humanity (Genesis 2:20-24; Mark 10:6-9). Marriage is the joining of one man and one woman into a lifelong relationship which the Scriptures call "one flesh." In this union the two retain their individual identities, but subordinate them to the larger relationship of marriage . . . . Marriage . . . [is a] covenant before God and state".

Along with upholding a high standard of marriage relationship, the church is prepared to support, guide, and provide resources for building and strengthening Christian homes. Those who are considering marriage should look to their pastoral leaders for counsel and instruction. Through the ministry of the church, God gives spiritual resources for marriages in trouble to bring healing and reconciliation. Those who find their marriage in crisis should not delay in seeking the counsel, support and guidance of the pastor and church.

This serious view of marriage does not rule out the possibility of separation or divorce but requires members who are faced with the threat to take counsel from the Word of God. Moreover, we believe that the possibility of marriage failure is reduced for those who see it as a covenant relationship and who pledge to conform themselves to God's will with regard to it, insofar as possible.

This, however, should not be seen as a word regarding any who were involved in a separation, divorce, or remarriage prior to their conversion to Christ. The pledge does not exclude them from membership. It is a self-evident fact that the church does not have disciplinary jurisdiction over the lives of any who are not members. But it has a God-given mandate to call its members to a high view of marriage and the home and to provide for the guidance and discipline of those members who become involved in a marriage breakup or look toward a remarriage after a divorce (see ¶A/341).

As Regards the Church

1. I have received Christian baptism.
Baptism is the rite of initiation into the visible church. It is one of two sacraments commanded by Jesus Christ (Matthew 28:18-20). Using the symbol of water, it signifies the washing away of sins and entrance into a new life. The church recognizes three modes of baptism--sprinkling, pouring, and immersion--and defers to the conscience of the individual believer regarding which mode is to be followed.

Our church holds to the propriety of the baptism of infants. This is reflected in Article XVII of our Articles of Religion: "Baptism is a symbol of the new covenant of grace as circumcision was the symbol of the old covenant; and, since infants are recognized as being included in the atonement, we hold that they may be baptized upon the request of parents or guardians who shall give assurance for them of necessary Christian training. They shall be required to affirm the vow for themselves before being accepted into church membership."

Baptism has been the subject of much controversy. Some communions hold that only those who are old enough to make a personal affirmation of faith may be baptized; others hold that it signifies God's covenant not only with an individual but with a family as well and, therefore, children are fitting subjects. It is held by some that there are three possible modes, while others contend for immersion as the only legitimate mode. The controversy continues, and opposing views are held by large Christian bodies only because the biblical evidence for either side is not conclusive.

The Free Methodist Church, with practically all other Christian communions (except the Salvation Army and Quakers), holds that baptism is the rite of entrance into the visible church. Our church has never been characterized by controversy over who is a fitting subject and what mode is most biblical. We have tried to subordinate the sacrament itself to the reality it signifies. And to prevent confusion, we affirm that uniformity is important both within a congregation and from area to area so as not to confuse people.

2. I accept the Articles of Religion and the authority of the Discipline in matters of church government.

No body, secular or sacred, can function effectively without some common ground of commitment. For this reason, every body, from the smallest club to the mightiest nation, establishes a constitution to which it asks its members to subscribe.

The church must include in its constitution some statement of doctrine or Articles of Religion touching on core convictions forged across many centuries and adhered to by our denomination from its beginning. Articles of Religion are not intended to be exhaustive.

In the Free Methodist denomination several congregations are incorporated into one conference and several conferences into a General Conference. This form of organization requires agreement on basic administrative procedures, and uniform procedures make for more efficient administration.

For these reasons, we ask all our members to accept the Articles of Religion and the authority of the *Book of Discipline* in matters of church government.

3. I will work for the advancement of God's kingdom and the mutual growth of fellow believers toward full stature in Christ in holiness and love.

The kingdom of God means the kingship or rule of God. This rule has been revealed to the world most fully in Jesus Christ. In Him, God's kingdom came in a unique way. In another sense, all who come under the rule of Jesus have a concern for the spread of His kingship. Paul spoke in the latter vein when he referred to certain colleagues among the Jews as "fellow workers for the kingdom of God" (Colossians 4:11).

Christian maturity brings with it a mounting desire to advance the Lord's work, to support evangelism and, in so far as possible, to participate in it, whether in our own community or in the remote regions of our world.

Our concern to advance Christ's kingly rule extends, however, not only to those who have not yet yielded to it. It includes, as well, a commitment to foster the mutual growth of fellow believers. "Full stature" is a metaphor for Christian maturity, a maturity that is to be characterized by Christian love (a moral quality), and Christian holiness (a religious quality of life).

4. I will seek to preserve the unity and witness of the church by nurturing and expressing Christlike love as described in 1 Corinthians 13.

It must be a great grief to our Lord Jesus Christ when bodies united by a common declaration of loyalty are rent with misunderstanding. When this happens, the church comes short of the spiritual unity made available to it by Christ's redeeming death and resurrected life. Its witness to the world is also marred, since the love that fellow believers bear one another is one of the most impressive marks of the true church to the world outside Christ.

In order for the "unity and witness" of the church to be preserved, it is necessary that serious Christians be committed to these objectives, consciously nurturing and openly practicing love of a special kind. This love is described in detail in 1 Corinthians 13.

5. I will cooperate in developing the Christian fellowship by willingness to receive and give counsel with tenderness and meekness; to pray for others; to aid others in sickness and distress; to cultivate Christian sympathy; and to show understanding, courtesy, and purity in all conversation.

The church is at heart a Christian fellowship, a community of believers who have been accepted by a redeeming God, and who, therefore, have agreed to accept one another. Fellowship is the willingness to know and be known. Unconditional acceptance assures Christians of personal worth and opens the way for growth. However, such fellowship is not automatic. It must be developed, and concerned Christians must cooperate in its pursuit.

The fellowship of the church can develop only where Christians are willing to share deeply in one another's lives. Their conversations will include words both of affirmation and counsel. If, for example, one Christian mars the fellowship by uncharitable conversation, another must counsel the erring one, "speaking the truth in love."

We pledge to be open to receive and give such counsel. However, it is to be received and given with tenderness--a carefulness not to give unnecessary offense; and with meekness--a disciplined spirit. When it comes to receiving counsel, we should be aware that we are not perfect specimens of God's grace, and our brothers and sisters are given to us to help us toward that goal.

With reference to giving counsel, a good rule of thumb to follow is this: if we have a strong desire to do so, we should refrain. When our inclination is to withhold but the Lord gently constrains us to speak, we should respond--with tenderness and meekness.

Prayer within the Christian fellowship lubricates relationships. Christians are uplifted when they know someone is praying for them. When the Christian community is functioning as God intends, the sick in the fellowship are visited and the distressed receive ministrations.

Christian sympathy--the ability to share the feelings of another--does not come about automatically. A Christian community is not achieved, moreover, by the mere development of techniques of relating. Such may lead only to the creation of sentimental ties. The fellowship is based on the historic revelation of God's love for sinners in Jesus Christ. "While we were still helpless, at the right time Christ died for the ungodly" (Romans

5:6, NASB). Upon this base, Christian feelings of mutual concern can be cultivated to maturity.

In our times, the word "conversation" refers largely to what is said. Used in the King James Version, the word refers to the *conduct of one's life*. Here are three great words to direct our conduct, including talk: understanding, courtesy, purity.

6. I will exercise responsible Christian stewardship by the careful and disciplined use of time, talents, and material resources, being sensitive to the needs of the church and my fellowmen. I will accept the biblical principle of tithes and offerings as the guide of my material stewardship and the support of the church. I will choose those activities which contribute to the spiritual, moral, intellectual, and physical well-being of myself and those who share in them.

Stewardship is the management of things not our own. We usually apply the word to money, but it encompasses much more. Strictly speaking, neither our treasures, talents, nor time are our own; God entrusts them to us to be managed for Him.

This part of the covenant reminds us of the biblical principle for the material support of God's work--tithes and offerings. The tithe is one-tenth of what God provides for us. The salaried worker should apply it to the gross of his income. The farmer or businessman cannot tithe the gross of all he handles, but he should seek to be equally generous in his calculations. Offerings are gifts we give beyond the tithe. The challenge of the stewardship of treasures is particularly important in affluent times.

Discipleship Means Commitment to a Group

One feature in the success of Weight Watchers is that the participants meet in groups. In doing so, they draw encouragement from one another. Their mutual commitments hold them to their diets in the interval between meetings. They know they must give an account. Solo dieters have a higher rate of failure because they lack the mutual support of a group.

In a wide range of activities requiring discipline, group commitment makes a difference. People who go to exercise clubs at set times at the YMCA or YWCA do better on the average than people who resolve to exercise every morning in their bedrooms. Door-to-door salesmen are often called to meetings in their district--in the company of other salesmen. This helps them by reinforcing their enthusiasm.

One may be a little bit religious on his own, but if he is a Christian who has caught a vision for discipleship, he must get in league with other Christians. Jesus himself singled out twelve men and made them His own group. Religious leaders across the centuries have done the same.

The Free Methodist Church provides for the formation of growth groups in every congregation. The *Book of Discipline* reads: "Christian growth groups should be formed within the congregation for the careful oversight of the members and the confirmation of seekers in the assurance of God's forgiveness in Christ. Membership in the groups ideally should be not more than twelve. A leader shall be chosen by the group, and the pastor may nominate. The groups should meet in a convenient location on a regular schedule.

"Group meetings should be devoted to meaningful creative prayer; the study of the Scriptures; the sharing of needs, aspirations, and victories; and fellowship in Christian love. Persons not yet believers should be invited into the fellowship as they desire to learn of Christ" (¶A/380).

The idea of encouraging discipleship by the use of groups is central in the history of Methodism. In the eighteenth century, converts were first formed into societies. These in turn were divided into classes of not more than twelve, with an appointed leader. So intense were the Wesleys in their desire to cultivate discipleship that they formed even more select bodies, called bands, and gave them instructions on the questions they were to ask of one another. The present growth groups are a continuation of the Methodist class meetings.

The need for this kind of close, committed fellowship is being felt again broadly across Christendom. Some groups have turned away disillusioned from the organized church and have formed independent face-to-face communities. By the thousands, home Bible studies have been organized and house churches formed. Within churches, small groups have come into being, sometimes with the blessing of the church, sometimes without. In the Free Methodist Church, growth groups are intended to be a part of the total function of the church, not a substitute for it.

If you are in the process of becoming a part of a growth group, here are some insights that may prove helpful to you.

1. *A Christian growth group is united by a fundamental commitment to God and one another.*

At the Free Methodist Church near where I live, a group of young professionals meets each Thursday night. They come together out of a world not sympathetic with Christian values. They are courageous people, but life has its stresses. The gathering is more helpful some weeks than others. What keeps it going is a commitment they made to each other at the outset: they would gather regularly and would miss only when necessity demanded. This faithfulness, like so many of life's important endeavors, is founded on commitment.

2. *Growth groups should be built around the Scriptures and should make all questions and concerns subject to them.*

If not, they can become merely experience-oriented and introspective, or they can even wander into heresy. Since they are under the auspices of the Free Methodist Church, the guidance of the pastor or the literature of the church should be sought in interpreting the Scriptures if differences arise.

3. *Growth without community is impossible.*

There may be exceptional situations, such as the lonely soldier at an outpost, without Christian fellowship, who must move ahead spiritually on his own. Even in his case, things go better if he is in correspondence with some Christian for mutual encouragement. When we are set on growing in Christ and increasing in Christian service, we will feel the need for commitment to a group.

4. *Growth groups are not perfect communities.*

The very fact that Christians become open to one another raises the possibilities for misunderstanding. There will be occasions when forgiveness must be sought and given. Reconciliation is at the heart of the Christian gospel. But the group gives opportunity for deeper acceptance than is to be found in the secular world. We are all more free to be open and grow when we know we are accepted for Christ's sake.

5. *Growth groups must allow for varying degrees of closeness.*

Some Christians are not used to sharing their thoughts and feelings. Others are not yet at the place where they can receive the ministrations of the group. In a growth group, each should be free to relate at the level of his present skills, and all should be under the restraints of the Spirit of Christ.

A Closing Word

Recently two young professional people dropped into my home for a visit. Both are Christians. Neither is a member of the Free Methodist Church, but both have the matter under consideration. What they expect of the church they join, they said, is a sense of clear commitment and mission.

This is a typical sentiment from Christians recently converted. These two belong to a new wave of believers who have been clearly awakened by the Spirit, who see the futility of life as lived at a secular level alone, and who want the church to be much more than an antiseptic version of a secular community.

In response to them, how can we do less than give ourselves wholeheartedly to Christ's church on earth?

For Review:
1. Indicate several aspects of Christian discipleship.

2. What is the purpose of the membership covenant?

3. State the four major divisions of the membership covenant.

4. What is the symbolic meaning of baptism? What three modes of baptism are recognized by the Free Methodist Church?

For Further Reading:
Book of Discipline, Free Methodist Church, 1989. Indianapolis, Indiana: Light and Life Press. Chapter III, "The Christian Life."

Demaray, Donald. *Snapshots: The People called Free Methodist*. Winona Lake, Indiana: Light and Life Press. (Light and Life Press now located in Indianapolis, Indiana.)

Marston, Leslie R. *From Age to Age a Living Witness.* Winona Lake, Indiana: Light and Life Press, 1960. Chapter 19, "Disciplined Living." (Light and Life Press now located in Indianapolis, Indiana.)

For Further Thought:

More than twenty affirmations comprise the membership covenant of the Free Methodist Church. Which requires the most discipline on your part to live by?

CHAPTER SEVEN

Mature Christian living is neither living without rules nor living by rules. It is living beyond rules. The rules set before us are gradually internalized. They become principles by which we regulate life. For example, the Wesleys in their general rules of 1742 required the early Methodists to "avoid evil of every kind" and included such specifics as "borrowing without a probability of paying; or taking up goods without a probability of paying for them." Such a rule would not long remain an external prohibition. It would become an internal principle, giving a quality of ethical excellence to the life of the person embracing it.

Living Beyond Rules

Does a denomination have an obligation to provide guidance for its membership in the form of clearly stated rules? I once set this question before a class of Christian college students.

All but one said yes. The dissenter argued that rules and regulations are unnecessary since Christians go directly to the Scriptures where they discover the standards they should set before themselves.

Vigorous discussion followed. One member asked his dissenting friend to estimate what percentage of Christians would in fact formulate their own rules from the Scriptures. Several figures were bandied about. The dissenter finally proposed 15 percent. Classmates asked him what obligation the church had to the other 85 percent. The discussion subsided and the class unanimously agreed that a church must provide guidance and discipline for its members.

Consider New Testament support for this idea. The first church council, held in Jerusalem about A.D. 50, produced the first disciplinary statement of the Christian church (Acts 15:19-20). It contained four important prohibitions which were delivered to all existing congregations.

By contrast, the Corinthian church was the freest of all New Testament churches, gauged by its own standards of freedom. It even prided itself in not disciplining members who sinned shamefully (1 Corinthians 5). Yet the Corinthian church is also the problem church of the New Testament.

The Apostle Paul made a clear connection between doctrine and duty. He believed one led naturally to the other, as all his letters show. The relationship between the two is especially clear in his Corinthian letters. He considered it unthinkable to leave this troubled church without clear guidance on how they should apply Christian doctrine to the regulation of their conduct. The New Testament epistles generally are statements which weave together doctrine and discipline. The apostles expected local congregational leaders to use their letters in promoting holy living.

Rules can help us. God gave the Ten Commandments to His

covenant nation Israel for their good. They were like ten basic rules for living. When they took them seriously, the nation benefitted religiously and morally.

Rules help us today by offering guidelines for our conduct. If we take them seriously, we train ourselves more quickly in right attitudes and conduct. Rules do not save us nor keep us saved, but they do offer us guidance in working out our salvation in fear and trembling.

However rules must be put in their rightful place. Mature Christians know you cannot live without rules any more than a truck driver can drive a truck or a manager can operate a store without special regulations. Mature Christians also know that it is folly to try to live by rules. To do so is to court legalism. For mature Christians it is neither a matter of living without rules nor by rules. The object is to live beyond rules.

Here's what this means. Rules help in laying a good foundation for the new life. But rules set down principles which are clear applications of Christian doctrine, and these we readily internalize. They become principles by which we regulate the new life in Christ.

For example, the Wesleys in their general rules of 1742, required the early Methodists to "avoid evil of every kind" and included such specifics as "borrowing without a probability of paying; or taking up goods without a probability of paying for them." Such a rule would not long remain an external prohibition. It would become an internal principle, giving a quality of ethical excellence to the life of the person embracing it.

Dealing with Matters on Which Christians Differ

But all this raises an interesting problem for new Christians. You will soon see that believers of apparently equal devotion nevertheless vary in their style of life. They also differ on the commitments they adopt. These differences can be explained in several ways. Christians perceive the implications of the gospel differently. Even such things as cultural background, personal temperament, and class differences can affect the way Christians work out the gospel in daily life. Of course, there are differences in degrees of devotion to take into account too.

This chapter will take up two areas of living in which Christians often differ in how they apply the gospel in personal life. First, there is the area of personal convictions: How do I decide what is right for me if no Christian absolute can be stated? Second, there is the area of the stewardship of money: How can I manage my material resources in such a way as to act out my devotion to Christ's cause? This is a call neither to live without rules nor by rules, but to come to that level of principled Christian living which is beyond rules. First, consider Christian convictions.

Christian Convictions

We do not apply the term conviction to moral absolutes. A Christian is not likely to say "I have a conviction against taking the Lord's name in vain." This is expressly forbidden in the Ten Commandments. We reserve the term *conviction* for areas in which Christians must make personal decisions on the basis of their best understanding of what righteousness requires. Because we apprehend truth with varying degrees of clarity, Christians differ in areas where the Scriptures do not speak explicitly.

How are we to know when our convictions are in line with the Scriptures? Romans 14 helps us. It gives us glimpses of two classes of people in the Roman church who were divided on matters of personal conviction. The Apostle Paul refers to one class as *weak in the faith* and the other as *strong*.

The ones who were weak in faith were overly conscientious. Today we might call them scrupulous. They were uneasy about foods which they thought should not be eaten by Christians and holy days which they thought should be kept. The *strong* considered these matters of no consequence.

In essence, the weak seemed to feel that their faith in Christ needed to be supplemented by scrupulous religious practices-- avoiding certain foods or keeping certain days. Their conviction about food and days, in turn, made them critical of the strong in faith. The strong in faith responded with mild arrogance toward their weaker brethren.

The issues themselves were not moral in nature, and this made the tension all the more difficult to deal with. They belonged in the realm of the amoral. That is, eating certain foods or refraining from them was not in itself a moral matter. But to certain individuals, it was a matter of conscience and thus became moral. The Apostle Paul sought to deal with the problem in such a way that the faith of neither weak nor strong was damaged while at the same time their love for each other was more mature.

In dealing with those two classes of Christians, the Apostle gave some excellent advice. We can take his advice and transpose it into questions which we can then use to help us formulate personal convictions. Here is how to make the most of the exercise: Think of some issue of conduct over which you may have had a great deal of uncertainty. Then, keep this issue in mind as you proceed. Here are the questions:

1. *Is my own mind clear?*
"Let everyone be fully convinced in his own mind . . . for whatever does not proceed from faith is sin" (Romans 14:5, 23, RSV).

Christians ought not to live in an unsettled frame of mind. When we are dealing with a question of conduct, it is not good for us to be on one side of the question one day and on the opposite side the next. Alternating from one position to the other, according to our company or surroundings, makes for spiritual instability. We must resolve the issue in such a way as to give us a fully settled mind, even though our decision may put us at variance with other equally committed Christians. No progress can be made so long as we are filled with doubts about things we do or avoid.

What is more, if we continue to do what can't be done in good faith, thus violating our conscience, we sin. This is the point made in Romans 14:23b. In seeking to form a clear conviction on some uncertain issue, we must come to the place where our own minds are fully convinced.

2. *Can I do this for the Lord?*
"If we live, we live to the Lord; and if we die, we die to the Lord. So then, whether we live or die, we belong to the Lord" (Romans 14:8).

When we confess faith in Jesus Christ, we acknowledge His lordship over our lives. It is no longer appropriate for us to say that what we do is our own business. Living under His lordship, everything we do is His business. This is clearly set forth in Romans 14:6-9.

With regard to what the Roman Christians should eat or refrain from, there was no clear-cut moral issue involved. Therefore, the Apostle Paul did not try to settle the problem in favor of either party. He simply reminded both sides about the lordship of Christ over all the Church and left them to ask concerning their specific problems, "Can I do this for the Lord?"

The question cannot be improved upon. Whenever uncertainty exists in the gray areas of life, our first concern is to resolve the uncertainty in favor of the lordship of Jesus Christ. This is more important than to find out what others are doing about the same matter, even though the example of other strong Christians may give us helpful direction. Without feeling arrogant toward those who refrain, or judgmental toward those who indulge, we must ask concerning the problem at hand, "How do I practice the lordship of Jesus Christ in this matter?"

3. *"When I consider this matter in the light of my coming appearance at the judgment seat of Christ, how do I feel about it?"*

"You, then, why do you judge your brother? Or why do you look down on your brother? For we will all stand before God's judgment seat . . . . So then, each of us will give an account of himself to God" (Romans 14:10, 12).

In the church in Rome, Christians with overly scrupulous consciences were judging and discrediting the faith of those who did not share their convictions about meats and holy days. In return, those with robust faith were looking with scorn on the weak, making light of what appeared to be foibles. This was not a healthy situation for it was creating division in the fellowship.

The Apostle's solution was to point both groups to the impending judgment seat of Christ. There was no need for one Christian to sit in judgment over another on these issues since both would one day have their lives properly evaluated at the judgment seat of Christ. Better for them both to regulate their own lives with this fact in mind than to judge or disdain one another.

When we must make a decision on any particular issue of conduct, it is hard to avoid asking, "What will my pastor think?" or, "What will my friends say?" Although their opinions have worth, for the formation of the highest convictions, we must learn to ask, "How will I feel about this on the day when I stand at the judgment seat of Christ to have my Christian life evaluated?"

4. *Will this be an offense to others?*

"It is better not to eat meat or drink wine or to do anything else that will cause your brother to fall" (Romans 14:21).

We Christians are members of a spiritual community--the Church--and the love of Christ we have experienced personally is also the bond of that community. We will not consciously want to do what is an offense to other members of Christ's community of love. Thus our decisions having to do with personal convictions will be made not only in terms of the lordship of Jesus Christ but also in terms of our responsibility to the weaker members of the Christian community.

This approach to the problem has its hazards. If all the strong Christians cater in their decisions to all the scrupulous Christians, the congregation may end up under the bondage of the weakest Christian of all, resulting in what has been called "the tyranny of the weak." Christian freedom is certainly threatened when a fellowship is regulated by the foibles of over-scrupulous members.

Even so, we must consider our brethren when we face problems of personal convictions. Mature Christians have often been known to leave some things out of their lives for no other reason than to avoid offending some weaker brother or sister. Such things as *meat* and *wine* are not so important to our well-being that we will put our own rights ahead of obligations to our brothers' faith, because a Christian community is of great worth.

Take note that the weak in faith must reason in this manner too.

The above questions may not completely solve the problem connected with the choosing of personal conviction. They are not intended to eliminate the personal struggle involved in becoming a moral person. Moreover, loopholes will be found in them by any who are not earnestly striving to do God's full will.

At the same time, they provide excellent guidelines for those who want assistance in areas where the Scriptures do not speak an explicit word. Think now of the problem you selected earlier. Put it under scrutiny of these four questions: (1) Is my own mind fully convinced? (2) Can I do this for the Lord? (3) In the light of my appearance at the judgment seat of Christ, how do I feel about this matter? (4) Will this be an offense to others?

Christian Stewardship

This brings us to the second area where Christians have to make highly personal decisions. This is the area of the management of material possessions for God. If God owns all things and only entrusts them to our care as His managers, how do we reflect our commitments by the way we use these resources?

When Abraham sent his servant Eliezer back to his country of origin to find a wife for his son Isaac, Eliezer was given complete freedom in the choice he made. It was not necessary for him to return to Palestine to get Abraham's or Isaac's final approval. He did not even have to send a courier back with a description of the woman he had chosen. This is in a sense surprising, since Eliezer was one of Abraham's slaves.

He was not just any slave, however. He had been with Abraham a long while and had become a trusted servant. He had been elevated and given the right to manage the affairs of Abraham's household, and on this mission he had full freedom to use his own judgment in choosing a daughter-in-law for Abraham. The Bible has a special title for this sort of servant. He was a *steward*.

To the present time, we talk about stewardship. It's a Christian doctrine drawn from both Testaments and is capable of adding zest and challenge to the life of anyone who embraces it.

In Bible times a steward was literally a person who administered the affairs of a house. He was entrusted with the full care of things not his own. In one of the many allusions Jesus made to stewards (Luke 12:41-48), it is clear that the three characteristics of a good steward are these: He understands his relationship to his lord and therefore carries out his assignment in faithfulness to him. He is left with considerable freedom in the management of the affairs under him and therefore the good steward is wise in seeing his opportunities and acting upon them. Finally, since nothing he works with is his own, the good steward carries on with the knowledge that he must give a final accounting to the owner.

These features are implicit in the words of Jesus: "Who then is the faithful and wise steward, whom his master will set over his household, to give them their portion of food at the proper time? Blessed is that servant whom his master when he comes will find so doing" (Luke 12:42-43, RSV).

Boredom must disappear from our lives when we begin to act as God's stewards. We are put in charge of things not our own, entrusted with their management every day, and called to deal with our stewardship with faithfulness and wisdom, knowing that we must give an account to God.

We can divide Christian stewardship into two broad areas. They are distinct from each other even though they overlap. Call them the stewardship of gifts of creation--the earth and all things in it--and gifts of redemption--the gospel of Jesus Christ and the spiritual gifts bestowed upon the Church.

Gifts of Creation

"The earth is the Lord's and everything in it, the world, and all who live in it; for he has founded it upon the seas, and established it upon the waters" (Psalm 24:1-2). This is a clear affirmation of God's ownership of all things, based upon Creation. Beginning at Genesis 1:1, the assumption runs throughout the Scriptures.

The story of Adam and Eve gives the first intimation of the doctrine of man's stewardship over the earth. The Lord placed the couple in Eden and put them in full charge but designated one tree in all the garden which they were not to touch. That one tree was a test of their willingness to be God's obedient stewards.

Mankind is still the steward of the earth. At the present time, we are being called by nature itself--and by God through nature--to give an account of our stewardship over its resources.

The culture of which we are a part is charged with being prodigal, wantonly using up a disproportionately large percentage of the resources entrusted to us. For two decades now we have been warned of the dire consequences that must soon ensue. Because of misuse, water supplies are threatened; and because of prodigal use, oil and other energy reserves are diminishing.

Should Christians have any distinctive response? The Free Methodist's focus on simplicity of life should come into its own here.

Our most immediate stewardship is the stewardship of our own bodies. These marvels of God's creation are imprinted with a dignity He himself has given and are ours to manage for Him. Yet secular prophets are constantly warning us of the damage we are doing our bodies by the misuse of drugs, overeating, and sedentary living.

There are ideologies that encourage us to be poor stewards, and we hear them every day. Materialism places an abnormally high value on things as ends in themselves. Consumerism pushes us to buy, spend, eat, use, discard, almost as a duty. Thrift is nearly antisocial. Hedonism teases us into placing a premium on pleasure and the good life, reinforcing us in our self-indulgent impulses. These ideologies are so carefully woven into our culture that we espouse them almost without realizing it.

As Christians, however, we must place over against these calls to prodigality the summons to stewardship. In a world heading into energy and resource crises, we ought to take the lead in demonstrating faithful and wise stewardship, carried out with a view to accountability, and be ready to show what this does to our style of life.

There is a direct connection between our stewardship of the earth and our stewardship of those possessions which pass through our own hands--our treasures. The teachings of Jesus are full of references to material possessions. His stories include such things as treasures hid in a field, pearls purchased at great sacrifice, pounds, talents, farms, inheritances. In His teachings, all these matters are concerns of stewardship. They are things to be managed and accounted for to their real owner--God.

When these ideas are worked out in our lives, we begin to

feel the challenge of managing the flow of our possessions to the glory of God. No one can be bored with life when this challenge possesses him.

In a sense, the tithing principle is a token of stewardship. When one sets aside 10 percent of his income for the Lord's work, he is symbolically stating that God is the owner of all his income and he is a manager. In times of spiritual decline, the people of God in the Old Testament withheld their tithes, thus showing that their sense of stewardship was waning. The prophet Malachi referred to this withholding as robbing God, the rightful owner (Malachi 3:8).

The management of possessions is important to the development of the Christian individually and to the church corporately. So important, in fact, that the Apostle Paul gave ample instructions to his churches, calling them to liberality in their giving. His instructions are most fully elaborated in 2 Corinthians 8-9. Here he refers to the giving of the churches in Macedonia as a manifestation of the grace of God. Grace stands for generosity in response to need, both on the part of God and His people (2 Corinthians 8:1).

One of the Apostle's most concentrated instructions on Christian giving is found in 1 Corinthians 16:2. Here he tells the Corinthian Christians to give in this fashion: "On the first day of every week, each of you is to put something aside and store it up, as he may prosper, so that contributions need not be made when I come" (RSV).

This little nugget deserves examination:

1. *Paul's instruction was first of all that Christian giving should be periodic: "on the first day of the week."*

Apparently by the time Paul wrote these words, Sunday, "the first day of the week," had become the day Christians met for the worship of their risen Lord. In contrast to the Jewish Sabbath, it was the Lord's Day. From verse 2 we may conclude that a regular part of the worship on that day was the giving and receiving of offerings, which in this particular case were to be sent to the poor saints in Jerusalem.

A professional man once asked me why a Christian may not write out a check once a month, or even once a year, and in this manner make his donation to the church. I replied that he certainly may do so for reasons of convenience, but this may cause him to miss a very important feature in the fabric of Christian worship. Giving is worship. Insofar as possible, the Christian should worship in giving on every Lord's Day.

As Free Methodist congregations come to see this worshipful feature of regular giving, they graduate from taking *collections* to giving *offerings*, and the mood of this part of the service changes from intermission to worship. Quite apart from the dimension of worship, you, an individual Christian, will be a much more effective steward in the long pull if you make generous giving a systematic part of your life. One Christian may impulsively give $500 to a special cause and stop with that, feeling good about his generosity. Another may systematically set aside $20 a week and give it regularly. At the end of the year, the systematic giver has given twice as much as the irregular giver. In the life of stewardship, there is room for both systematic and spontaneous generosity.

2. *Christian stewardship should also be personal: "each of you."*

When Paul addressed this passage to "each of you," it is apparent that he expected giving to involve the whole congregation. From this we may draw helpful inferences.

The main wage earner in the family should represent the family in giving, of course. But if this is done quite privately and on behalf of the family, it may deprive other members of the family of the joyful sense of the stewardship of dollars. Every earner in the family may worship in giving. Young people should learn the stewardship of money with their first earnings. Even children can treat their allowance as a trust from God and so be taught early to gain experience as His managers.

All this is consistent with Paul's exhortation, that everyone was to lay by him in store for the Sunday offering. Practiced literally, this lifts all Christians in a congregation into the elevated experience of the management of God's possessions for God's glory. In the church where this happens, there are ample funds to meet all needs in a distinctly Christian way.

3. *In the third place, Christian giving should be provident: "put something aside and store it up."*

Provident giving is planned in advance. Advanced planning in this manner makes giving a deliberate act of worship. One attends public worship to give as well as to receive.

The Corinthian Christians had to decide by the week what they could give, because their meager income differed from one week to the next. In modern times, income has generally become more stabilized. Plans for the stewardship of dollars can be made providently by the month or the year and reflected in a pledge made to a yearly church budget. However these details are cared for from place to place, the happiest Christians are those who live with a real sense of stewardship and act out that stewardship by the planned and purposeful giving of their means.

4. *In the fourth place, giving should be proportionate: "as he may prosper."*

According to Paul, each Christian was to set aside his weekly offering in accordance with his prosperity. Prosperity, of course, is a subjective thing. A person whose heart overflows with thankfulness to God may look upon a meager salary as abundant, while another Christian not so blessed with the spirit of gratitude may feel impoverished with twice as much. Nevertheless, each must give a portion consistent with his prosperity.

Proportionate giving should begin with a tithe. Nowhere in the Bible is less than a tithe suggested. In fact, the tithe is commanded in the Old Testament and commended in the New. Jesus rebuked the Pharisees for being meticulous about tithing while at the same time being indifferent about showing mercy. He concluded by saying, "These (the tithing of mint and dili and cummin) you ought to have done, without neglecting the others" (Matthew 23:23b, RSV).

Tithing is a method of giving which is deeply rooted in the Scriptures and highly commended by those who have practiced it; yet the stewardship of money does not end with the giving of a tithe. All money is a trust from God. When God begins to prosper us so that we have more than the essentials of life, we must ask what the principle of proportionate giving is to mean now. Our giving is always subject to adjustment; and as God prospers us beyond basic needs, that adjustment should be upwards. Someone has said, "When a man begins to prosper, either the Lord gets a steward or the devil gets a soul."

5. *Finally the Christian giving should be preventive: "So that contributions need not be made when I come."*
These words of the Apostle to the Christians in Corinth had to do with a gift of money they were to make for the poor saints at Jerusalem. His last word of advice was that their giving was to be systematic and proportionate in order to avoid the emergency gatherings at the time of his impending visit. "On the first day of every week, each of you is to put something aside and store it up, as he may prosper, so that contributions need not be made when I come" (1 Corinthians 16:2, RSV).

He was concerned to prevent sub-Christian methods of giving. This first-century principle can help us in our stewardship of dollars today.

Sometimes appeals are made in church to meet deficits or other obligations. A loan payment may be due or missionary giving may have lagged. Such appeals often stimulate an admirable show of generosity. But this burst of generosity never quite conceals the fact that budgetary emergencies usually arise because the church has been giving in a sub-Christian fashion. It is a good thing to take time from a Sunday morning worship service to catch up in the payment of pledges; it is better to take time every Sunday to practice preventive giving. Careful and glad-hearted stewardship will make the difference.

Such giving need not rule out special offerings. In fact, it will clear the way for noble and generous response to appeals that take God's people beyond immediate congregational commitments. Such preventive giving, in fact, will open up new vistas of the stewardship of money, freeing us to respond to them as they come.

Gifts of Redemption

As growing Christians, we dare not stop with the stewardship of the gifts of creation, exciting as such stewardship is. The stewardship of the gifts of redemption presents us with an equally great challenge.

1. *The Gospel*

The gospel itself is given to the church as a stewardship. It is, in fact, the greatest stewardship responsibility we have. In 1 Corinthians 2, (RSV) the gospel is declared to be "God's secret wisdom." In 1 Corinthians 4:1, the Apostle calls himself and those who serve with him, "servants of Christ and stewards of the mysteries of God," adding that "it is required of stewards that they be found trustworthy."

We can infer from this that the world will never stumble onto the gospel nor come to understand it naturally. To many it is foolishness. Therefore the stewardship of the church is to propagate the gospel in such a manner that God's way of saving mankind will be made known through his stewards of the gospel. This idea is supported by the Great Commission (Matthew 28:18-20), by parables of Jesus (Matthew 25:14-30), and by the example of the apostles and the early church.

What may we expect to happen to us today when we see the gospel as a foremost stewardship? The insight will drive us back to the New Testament again and again to deepen our understanding of the mystery. Moreover, we will want to experience it ever more fully, being dissatisfied to stop with an initial experience of salvation. We'll want this stewardship to show itself in all concerns of the church, and we'll begin to pray regularly for every effort made to send the gospel forth in the community. There will be a special concern that ministers be called forth from the new generation of Christians.

2. *Spiritual Gifts*

Another dimension of the stewardship of the gifts of redemption has to do with the exercise of spiritual gifts. Writing to the Christians of the dispersion, Peter exhorted, "Each one should use whatever gift he has received to serve others, faithfully administering God's grace in its various forms" (1 Peter 4:10). He had in mind here the stewardship of gifts within the ministry of the church. He said, "If anyone speaks, he should do it as one speaking the very words of God. If anyone serves, he should do it with the strength God provides (v. 11). The object of this stewardship is not left in doubt. Gifts are to be exercised as a stewardship "so that in all things God may be praised through Jesus Christ" (v. 11).

The subject of gifts has been more controversial than it needs to be. Gifts have been overemphasized in some cases and misused in others. They have thus been a source of dispute and factiousness, as they were in the church at Corinth.

None of these problems, however, should obscure the fact that God himself gives gifts to His people for the upbuilding of the Church. There are four separate lists of gifts in the New Testament; two in 1 Corinthians 12, one in Romans 12, and one in Ephesians 4. These are in addition to the abbreviated list of two gifts mentioned by Peter. Someone has calculated that in the New Testament 21 gifts in all are listed.

From the teachings of 1 Corinthians 12, we can affirm the following truths about gifts: God's gifts are grace-gifts, generously bestowed by God and always referring honor back to Him rather than to the person on whom they are bestowed. They are not for personal display. Gifts are given to Christians by the sovereign Spirit, and the dispersal of gifts rests with Him. Gifts are for the upbuilding of the church, not for the enhancement of the reputation or visibility of the persons exercising them. The highest gift is love, universally available to all Christians and necessary to the effective functioning of all other gifts.

The Apostle Peter's distinctive statement is that God's gifts to the church are varied and we are to be good stewards of them. We should therefore all be concerned to discern what gift or gifts we may have been given. If we raise this question in humility, the church itself can help us. Our concern should then be to use our gifts faithfully, wisely, and with a view to our final accounting to God.

A spiritual gift is a *charisma*. That means it is a free gift, given by God to one of His children for use in the church and in the world. There are many grace gifts. Here is a little exercise based on 1 Peter 4:10-11 for you to use in considering your gifts.

1. Based on verse 10, should every congregation have a small company of gifted people at its center? How many members of your congregation should have a gift for ministering?

2. Whatever the gifts, however varied, what is the function of every gift the Spirit gives to members of the church?

3. Based on the last half of verse 10, when you exercise your gift in the service of others in the Christian family, what are you doing?

4. Verse 11 names two large categories of gifts. These are categories into which all spiritual gifts should be divided. Take a sheet of paper and place a vertical line through the center making two columns. Write the name of one of these categories at the top of each of the columns. Arrange the following gifts under one of the two headings: preaching, administering the finances of the church, serving tables, caring for the sick, prophesying, teaching, giving of one's means, offering words of wisdom.

5. Think about your gift. Which category does it fall under? If you are not sure, here is a way you can help to discover which category it falls into. Talk with two or three mature Christians--a pastor, a Sunday school teacher, a devout Christian--and ask their opinion. God often teaches us what He wants us to know through the advice of other Christians.

6. Consider how you might put your gift to greater use. You may seize opportunities for speaking or Christian service that are already being put before you but which you have not yet acknowledged. Watch to see what opportunities present themselves. Or you may offer yourself to your pastor or a department of your church--the Sunday school, the visitation team. When you do, trust those you offer yourself to to have good judgment. Accept whatever opportunities come, however large or modest.

7. Remember that serving Christians are happier Christians. When you exercise a gift, it tends to become more effective.

A Closing Word

The material in this chapter may have seemed to you wide-ranging--rules, convictions, stewardship. How can they be connected?

In this manner: Mature Christians live beyond rules, and

hence they differ from one another in some convictions they hold and in the stewardship they practice. Some Christians seem to live more simply than others and some are more generous than others.

These differences would not need to exist if we could draw up a list of rules so comprehensive that nothing would be left unregulated. That would be pure legalism and unworkable besides. Differences would also not need to exist if we could dispense entirely with standards of expectation, letting grace become a substitute for moral living. That would be antinomianism.

The Free Methodist position is as follows: Let us use a membership covenant to highlight those issues of worship and conduct on which we want our people to stand together. But let this be in the nature of rules for beginners, and let us hope that these rules will become internalized as principles.

At the same time, let us recognize that salvation is by grace through faith. Nothing we can do can increase our merit with God. All merit is in Jesus Christ who has given His life for our full redemption. Hence, we can be completely dependent on His grace while at the same time responsive to the church's call to live lives of Christian excellence.

Wherever the subject of stewardship is touched on in the Scriptures, the thought of final judgment is not far from sight. In the judgment, all differences are to be resolved. Paul speaks to Christians when he writes, "We shall all stand before the judgment seat of Christ."

When we realize that we must be judged by Christ, we are reluctant to judge our brothers and sisters in the church today. At the same time, the truth of final judgment spurs us to live lives of balanced conviction and ardent stewardship.

For Review:
1. Distinguish between living without rules and legalism.

2. Based on Paul's writings in Romans 14, what are the four questions Christians may use in formulating their personal convictions?

3. State the two broad categories of our stewardship as Christians.

4. What five instructions regarding giving are found in 1 Corinthians 16:2?

5. What is the highest gift?

For Further Reading:
Read Romans 12-15, noting all moral instructions given to Christians.

List the areas of your life that should be brought under a stronger sense of stewardship.

What is your special gift? How can you be a better steward of it?

For Further Thought:

List all the areas of your life that you can think of that should be brought under a stronger sense of stewardship.

What is your special gift or gifts? How can you be a better steward of it (them)?

CHAPTER EIGHT

Physical life is not self-sustaining. It relies for its continuance on resources outside itself. Thus, the normal development of an infant is dependent upon regular supplies of food and oxygen, as well as loving association with other humans.

Spiritual life functions under somewhat the same laws. Its continuance and development are also dependent upon resources outside itself. Specifically, it is dependent upon the grace of God, and for this reason the Christian must learn how God's grace is appropriated to his life.

Practices That Nurture

Wedding vows, however solemnly recited, do not guarantee a happy marriage. That is not to say they are not important, but only that of themselves they are not enough.

In the same way, for Christians, membership covenants have value, but of themselves they cannot guarantee a rich and satisfying Christian life. They serve as guidelines, not as sources of energy.

The satisfying Christian life is rooted in God himself and energized by His grace. Even this must not be taken to mean that grace is some substance separate from God which He dispenses to us. Grace is God himself acting toward us with undeserved generosity. He does not treat us as our sins deserve but with a largess such as only He can display.

The Means of Grace

Physical life is not self-sustaining. It relies for its continuance on resources outside itself. Thus, the normal development of an infant is dependent upon regular supplies of food and oxygen, as well as loving association with other humans.

Spiritual life functions under somewhat the same laws. Its continuance and development are also dependent upon resources outside itself. Specifically, it is dependent upon the grace of God, and for this reason the Christian must learn how God's grace is appropriated to his life.

Here, the term, "means of grace," comes in. It suggests practices by which God's grace is appropriated. These means are indicated in the Scriptures, and the Christian church has given careful instruction on how they are to be used. Principally, they are the Bible, prayer, Christian fellowship, and the sacrament of the Lord's Supper.

As we consider them, it will be well to keep in mind that although God has providently set before us these means of His grace, it is up to us how effectively we use them.

The Bible, the Christian's Handbook

How does the Christian settle questions involving what he

should believe or how he should live? Obviously, he must have some authority to which he turns for direction in these matters. His future hinges on his choice at this point. What is the ultimate authority for Christians?

In Christendom generally, at least three answers are put forth. Some say reason should be the final arbiter in matters of faith and conduct. The experience of the church and the pronouncements of the Scriptures are not to be overlooked; but when things come to an issue, human reason will speak the last word. Those who hold this opinion are usually referred to as Liberals (in a theological sense).

The ultimate authority for others is the church, viewed as an ecclesiastical organization. Reason has a place, and the Bible is not spoken of lightly; but when matters come to an issue, they both bow to the dogmas and decrees of the church. Roman Catholicism is the best illustration of this point of view.

Still others look to the Bible to speak the last word on matters of faith and conduct. It is regarded as the inspired Word of God, and hence as the ultimate authority in setting forth what men should believe and how they should live. The term Conservative, used in a theological sense, best describes those of this persuasion.

The Free Methodist Church falls in this third class. As a church we recognize the value of enlightened reason, and we discourage any disparagement of its use in seeking to understand the will of God. At the same time, we believe the unaided intellect cannot be our ultimate authority--for two reasons. First of all, it is undependable, being impaired by the Fall. Besides this, it is inadequate to tell us all we want to know about God and the hereafter. Thus, for us, the Bible must stand above reason.

As a denomination, we also believe strongly in the corporate value of the church to guide, discipline, and nourish its members. But we hold that throughout history the Bible has stood above the church, not the church above the Bible.

Therefore, while recognizing the proper place of reason and the church, we believe that the Bible is the reliable Word of God and must speak the last word on matters of faith and conduct. If reason is at variance with the Scriptures, reason must be corrected; if the church is in disagreement with the Scriptures, the church must realign itself.

But caution is necessary at this point. The ultimate authority to which we direct our people is not a closed Bible. Nor is it a Bible to which they may resort only for proof-texts or ammunition in religious debate. It is not even the Bible as an object to be revered. It is rather an open Bible, regularly studied, a veritable handbook for Christian living.

We seek, in fact, to lead our people to use their Bibles daily in an enlightened fashion. Those who bring the most to the Scriptures by way of a prepared heart and head will take the most from them. For this reason, three counsels are now given which should assist you to use the Bible as a daily means of grace.

First of all, *learn to think realistically about the Bible.*

Think of the Bible in a twofold light. It is at the same time a book with a human history and a book with a divine origin. Neither aspect in itself gives the whole picture. To see either aspect separately is likely to lead to a shallow or false view of the sacred Scriptures. But when we view them together, we are confronted with the majesty and the mystery of this book.

The human history of the Bible is a fascinating story. The book as we have it today comes from the pens of at least forty different authors. These range from desert-bred men like Amos to those of aristocratic bearing like Isaiah. Its sixty-six books span at least fourteen centuries from the earliest writing to the last. They were penned in Hebrew, Greek, and Aramaic.

During the early centuries these writings were copied and recopied, one manuscript at a time, by the painstaking efforts of faithful scribes. Some were recorded on papyrus, some on the skins of animals. These were multiplied into thousands of copies, any of which were lost or destroyed, though some still exist today.

In the middle of the fifteenth century of our era, the first full book produced by the newly invented printing press was a Bible. The printing press then introduced something of a revolution. First it made the Bible available in Latin, a little later in Greek, and finally in the English language.

Different translations appeared one after another as the book was put into the language of the people. The best known of these was the *King James Version*, published in 1611. It soon became the most popular of them all, pushing the others from the field by its sheer superiority. In 1982 an updated *New King James Version* was published. Slight changes in spelling, wording and format make this version more readable for people today.

Our century has been another period of multiplied translations. Because these have been based on more ancient and trustworthy manuscripts unearthed since the seventeenth century, we are closer than modern man has ever been before to accurate records of the Scriptures as they were originally penned.

The *Revised Standard Version* led the way in this latest outpouring and came under fierce attack for poorly founded reasons. Ironically, it has turned out to be one of the more conservative translations and close to the *King James Version* of which it is a revision. It is gradually winning the widest acceptance among those who want faithfulness to the original language, conservative use of the English language, and an idiom that falls comfortably on North American ears.

The *New International Version* was released in the early 1970's. Because of its clear expression, contemporary language forms and high readability; it has been adopted as the translation of choice for Christian education ministries, church curriculum, and general use.

Many who know the history of the sacred Scriptures--the countless fascinating events which attended their dissemination, and the numerous manuscripts, copies, fragments, and translations that exist--never cease to wonder. They marvel at the surprising unanimity which exists among them in essential points. No other collection of writings has been preserved with such amazing care.

The reason for this, we believe, is that the Bible has not only a human history but also a divine origin. It constitutes a revelation from God, an unfolding, that is, of divine truth which man does not have the capacity to discover by himself. It was given to man, we further believe, by the inspiration of God. That is, the Holy Spirit so moved the hearts and minds of chosen men that they were able to record these sacred truths faithfully and pass them on to posterity (2 Timothy 3:16).

We believe that the Holy Spirit has so preserved these truths across the ages that in spite of the complex and fascinating history of the Bible, it is utterly dependable in its teachings regarding what we must believe and how we should live. While its human history gives it breadth and warmth as literature, its divine origin gives it authority. Christians who realistically come to grips with both these facts are likely to hold the deepest respect for this God-breathed book.

Second, *learn the unifying pattern of the Bible.*

Those who decide to take the Bible seriously sometimes come away from their earliest encounters quite discouraged. It seems vast. Complex. Mysterious. Such an impression can be traced usually to a failure to see that the Bible is not so much a book as a library of sixty-six books.

In the same manner, let a newcomer plunge into the heart of a great city, and he is likely to come up with the same feeling of vastness and incomprehensibility. Where does this street go? Why is that avenue on such a strange angle? What a vast complex of buildings, lanes, and boulevards!

Let the same newcomer first be introduced to the overall layout of the city by use of a clear and simple map. Let him fix the pattern in his mind. Then one particular section will not be so confusing, for in his mind he will see it in relation to the city as a whole.

It is much the same with the Bible. One who plans to take it seriously will be rewarded for the time spent in mastering the overall pattern of the book. It does have an unmistakable plan. This can be seen first of all in its division into the Old and New Testaments. Beyond that it can be outlined into seven major divisions as follows:

1. *The Historical Books* record the rise and fall of God's chosen people, the Hebrew nation. Beginning with Genesis and concluding with Esther, seventeen books unfold God's dealings with a nation chosen for His own purpose. How the nation came to be is an inspiring story. Its consolidation, its fortunes and misfortunes, its religious failure, and the consequent judgment are all a part of this many-sided account. These early books contain the foundation for all later revelation and therefore they are an indispensable part of the sacred Scriptures.

2. *The Poetical Books* contain literature from the golden age of the chosen nation. Israel came to its highest hour nationally during the times of David and Solomon. The majority of the literature in the five poetic books--Job through the Song of Solomon--belong to this era. As literature, this material is unexcelled. But it is included in the canon of the Old Testament because it is a part of the unfolding message of redemption. This fact is especially seen when we observe that any of its passages are cited again in the New Testament and are referring there to the Messiah (Psalm 2:7; Acts 3:33; Psalm 16:10; Acts 2:27; Psalm 118:26; Matthew 21:9).

3. *The Prophetic Books* are composed of literature from the nation's dark days. After the reign of Solomon, national decline set in for the Hebrew nation. It was gradual, and it was related specifically to the nation's failure to honor its covenant with God. At this time, God commissioned prophets to speak His word to an unfaithful people. One after another they pled with Judah and Israel to repent of their backslidings and return to obedience to God. Things went from bad to worse, however; and finally, as a direct judgment of God, the Northern Kingdom was carried into captivity. Later the same end befell the Southern Kingdom.

Some of the prophetic literature, such as Hosea, was written before the captivity. Some, such as Ezekiel, was produced while the Hebrew people were away from their land. And some belong to the times of the return from the captivity. The last three Old Testament prophets are in this latter class.

4. *The Gospels* introduce us to the man whom the nation produced. The word, gospel, means good news. The New Testament opens on this note. Four different accounts are given of the incarnation of God in human history in the person of Jesus Christ. That God had raised up a nation is evident in the Old Testament accounts. Although that nation had sensed in its noblest moments that it was to be an instrument in God's hand, it had failed. This failure notwithstanding, God had kept His promise and, from the seed of Abraham, had given to the world a Savior.

5. *The Acts of the Apostles* shows us how the reign of the Messiah among all nations begins. This document is the first

history of the Christian church. Beginning with an account of the supernatural origin of the Christian church at Pentecost, it covers approximately thirty years and follows the disciples on their mission to make Christ known from Jerusalem to Rome. The church in the New Testament, the spiritual Israel, is appointed to fulfill the ministry of world evangelization at which physical Israel had failed (Acts 1:8; 1 Peter 2:9). This book shows us how the church began such a mission.

6. *The Epistles* contain the teachings and principles of the one whom God had sent. This section of literature includes twenty-one letters written during the infancy of the church. Some were written to young congregations, others to individuals. The major writers are Paul, John, and Peter. They deal thoroughly with the centrality of Christ in the life of the individual and the church, and they develop the ethics of Christian living deriving from His lordship.

7. *The Revelation* forecasts Christ's universal dominion. This last book of the Bible is the distinctly prophetic book of the New Testament. Whereas Genesis begins with the creation of the heavens and the earth, this book concludes with the promise of the new heavens and the new earth. The one message it sets forth throughout is the triumph of Christ in human history, and on this note it fittingly closes the Book of God.

Look back across these seven divisions to see how they reveal the unfolding purpose of God in history. In doing so you will also be aware that the Bible is a library of sixty-six books, all of which are unified by the one developing theme: the redemption of the world by Christ Jesus. The Christian will profit by memorizing such a simple outline as this and then by going on to match up the relevant Bible books with each division. This will prove to be only a first step toward a more thorough acquaintance with the Word of God.

Third, *build the message of the Bible into your life.*

No Christian will question the need to see the great value of coming to understand the overall plan of the Christian Scriptures. But evaluation and understanding are not enough. They are in a sense only preliminary. Beyond them one must learn how to make the Bible a living part of his life. He must learn to assimilate its truth until it becomes a part of the warp and woof of his living. God wishes His Word to be etched on the fleshly tables of believers' hearts.

What simple directions can we follow to bring this to pass?

1. *Have a set time each day to turn to the Word of God for direction or strength.*

Just as a company of soldiers gets its marching orders before the march, and an orchestra tunes its instruments before the concert, so the Christian should turn to the Scriptures and prayer before the day begins in earnest. Prayer is the Christian's way of tuning in for a harmonious day, and the Scriptures contain each day's marching orders.

That this should be done at the beginning of the day is beyond question. The psalmist said, "My voice shalt thou hear in the morning, O Lord; in the morning will I direct my prayer unto thee, and will look up" (Psalm 5:3, KJV). To his voice, a thousand great Christians have said, "Amen"; and you will too if you once learn the value of starting the day by turning to the Bible for a daily portion.

2. *Develop and follow a plan in your Bible reading.*

Some have found it profitable to read one chapter a day from the Old and one from the New Testament. Some prefer to read more from the New than from the Old. In any event, read consecutively (don't play hopscotch in the Scriptures!), and stay with each book until you have finished it. Some portions (the begats of Matthew 1, for example) will not be as inspiring as others, in which case you will not spend much time with them. But keep in mind that they are part of the total picture and, thus, not without meaning.

Let your plan include the use of other tools as well. A study Bible is a good investment, and pencil and paper are invaluable. Use the pencil to mark special passages and to write down thoughts that the Lord gives you as you pour over His Word. Besides, it's surprising what having a pencil poised to write can do for concentration.

You should plan also to seek each morning for at least one verse that you can take with you into the day. Though it takes only half an hour to eat a meal, it takes two hours to digest and assimilate that food until it is a part of you. The same principle applies to the Scriptures. They must be assimilated by recollection and meditation.

Your plan should also include some memorization. Memorize the books of the Bible. Then begin to memorize verses that speak especially to you. You will soon be committing to memory passages you can use in soul winning. This has been the practice of many great Christians.

You will work out a plan that suits your way of thinking, but be sure it is a plan which you can follow. For a start, let it include three activities: mark, memorize, and meditate. If you take this procedure seriously, you will find the Scriptures to be a comfort in sorrow, a shield in temptation, and a sword in conflict.

3. *Finally, obey the Word as it speaks to you.*

It is important always to remember that God reveals His secrets not so much to the quick-witted as to the honest-hearted. Disobedience to God and a love of the Scriptures cannot exist together. The Bible rebukes disobedience, or disobedience closes the book. Therefore, it is wise to begin the time of devotions with a prayer such as this, "Search me, O God, and know my heart: try me, and know my thoughts: and see if there be any wicked way in me, and lead me in the way everlasting" (Psalm 139:23-24, KJV).

Prayer, the Christian's Means of Communion with God

Prayer, the second means of grace, is a subject so vast that only some of its practical aspects can be considered here. It is a strange paradox that although in every human breast there is something like an instinct for prayer, at the same time the cultivation of an effective prayer life demands resolute purpose and faithful perseverance. We must keep this before us as we look at two important truths which you will take seriously if you wish to use prayer effectively.

First, *consider four different ways in which the Christian may engage in prayer.*

1. *Mental prayer.* This is simply the act of turning the heart Godward in the midst of life's activities. The full use of mental

prayer was no doubt in Paul's mind when he said to the Thessalonians, "Pray without ceasing" (1 Thessalonians 5:17, KJV). Those who have learned this habit have found it possible to pray at chores, on the way to school, while doing the dishes, or wherever they happen to be.

2. *Private prayer.* This signifies the quiet time which usually follows the reading of the Scriptures--that time each day when the Christian draws apart from the press of things to be alone with his Lord. It is an obedient response to Jesus' words to "Enter into thy closet, and when thou hast shut thy door, pray to thy Father which is in secret . . ." (Matthew 6:6, KJV).

Mental prayer is not enough. The Christian must add to it daily seasons when activities cease and he takes a time to be holy. But such a discipline is not without reward. "Thy Father which seeth in secret shall reward thee openly" (Matthew 6:6, KJV), was Jesus' assurance. This means that the Christian's life of secret prayer is his most poorly kept secret.

3. *Family prayer.* Wherever this is practiced, it is a wholesome boon to the home. Family prayer recognizes that the home is a religious institution with a religious center. Family prayer, conducted daily, accents the spiritual meaning of life. It builds into the thinking of children a consciousness that God is near in everyday affairs. Such prayer is a cohesive force for the whole family and is therefore an essential part of a strong Christian home.

Family devotions need be neither long nor tedious. They may center in the Scriptures by the reading of a short portion, the passing of a promise box, or the recitation of favorite verses. Prayer may be led by a particular member of the family each time or each may pray in turn if the prayers are kept short. But it is important that the occasion be more than a ritual. It should never lose the note of importance and the atmosphere of spiritual delight.

4. *Public prayer.* New Christians find an amazing source of strength in praying with other Christians. And mature Christians in a church never progress to the point where group prayer is unnecessary as an aid to holy living.

Our churches, therefore, provide in the midweek prayer service and other group meetings an opportunity to learn to participate in public prayer. For new Christians, the group should be small and composed of sympathetic believers. Some pastors divide their prayer meeting congregation into smaller cells of six or so for the prayer time in order to involve the whole congregation in the practice of prayer.

Of the four ways in which the Christian may participate in prayer, this is without doubt the hardest for the new believer. It will test his nerve in most cases. But as he is gently and sympathetically assisted, he is introduced to a rewarding prayer experience. And if the practice is developed early in the Christian life, it will help him to be a strong and radiant Christian.

Now, *consider the elements which make up a well-rounded prayer.*

When Christians complain about a sense of unreality in prayer, it may be because they lack adequate forms for prayer. To correct such a problem, it is wise to understand the five elements of prayer. The sequence presented below may not be best for every believer, but it constitutes a useful pattern with which to begin.

1. *Adoration.* Quieting the mind before God at the outset of prayer is time well spent. This may best be done by beginning prayer with adoration. But how should one go about it?

The Psalms present passages which lift the eyes heavenward in humble adoration. For example, "The Lord reigneth, he is clothed with majesty; the Lord is clothed with strength, wherewith he hath girded himself..." (Psalm 93:1, KJV). Ponder that and let the majesty and sovereignty of the Eternal One fill the mind at the outset of prayer.

The hymnbook too affords assistance in bringing the supplicant into the spirit of adoration:

> *Jesus, the name high over all,*
> *In hell, or earth, or sky;*
> *Angels and men before it fall,*
> *And devils fear and fly.*

Whatever method one uses to create the attitude, adoration should mark the opening of prayer in the secret closet. It centers the mind on God. It tunes the heart for communion and stimulates faith by recognizing the greatness of the one to whom we pray. It tends to turn the attention away from the immediate distractions of life.

Adoration, therefore, fittingly opens the time of prayer.

2. *Confession.* Confession should find a place in every prayer, and it is important to think distinctly about what it involves. On the one hand, confession can become routine and even glib. Such has often happened when a prayer is formally closed with the remark, "This we ask along with the forgiveness of our sins." Confession of wrongdoing in a routine fashion like this is likely to add insincerity to the list of sins.

On the other hand, it is an equally great hazard to conclude that because we are saved there is nothing to confess. The Christian who has caught a glimpse of the holiness and love of God will not be slow to confess his unworthiness. Nor will he be tardy in confessing his mortal weakness and his omissions. Often the impassioned prayer of the psalmist will tumble from his lips, "Cleanse thou me from secret faults"--faults hidden not from God or others, but from himself. And if he has knowingly sinned, he will be quick to confess and forsake that sin in the light of 1 John 2:1-2.

The question may arise, "How is such instruction consistent with perfect love?" The answer is that the doctrine of perfect love proclaims the glorious fact that one *need* not sin, not that one *cannot* sin. There is a significant difference. The life of perfect love is lived only by constant vigilance against sin. Therefore, if one slips from the truth that he need not sin to the error that he cannot sin, he is likely to develop a serious blind spot regarding his own life.

Furthermore, perfect love does not assure the Christian against errors of judgment and, with that, possible unintentional errors of conduct. Because he knows this, he will always be ready to confess to God and his fellowman. He will never in this life find himself above the need to pray, "And forgive us our debts, as we also have forgiven our debtors" (Matthew 6:12, RSV). In fact, Christians must pray this prayer meaningfully to be kept from pride, harshness of spirit, and a score of other wrong attitudes which may subtly overtake those who lose sight of the fact that the treasure of grace is in an earthen vessel.

3. *Petition*. Confession leads naturally to petition which is the practice of a needy child in the presence of a loving father. Petition is personal request, and because God is Father, the Christian will see that no personal request is too great or too small to be presented.

However, here again a word of caution is in order. The Christian is invited to pray, "Give us this day our daily bread" (Matthew 6:11, RSV). He is urged, "Ask, and you will receive, that your joy may be full" (John 16:24b, RSV). He is assured, "If you ask any thing in my name, I will do it" (John 14:14, RSV). These promises give grounds for great confidence in prayer. At the same time, if prayer begins and ends in petition, it will die. Petition is only one element in prayer, and so we must move to yet another.

4. *Intercession*. In petition, the Christian makes personal requests. In intercession he goes before God on behalf of another. Intercession involves three or more persons, and many times it becomes the highest point in prayer. To make petition the end of prayer is to make prayer into a selfish thing. But to go beyond this to intercession introduces the Christian to a ministry in which he can very well lose himself in the concerns of others.

Many Christians keep a prayer list. At the time of intercession the list brings to mind the needs of others for which they are to intercede. Those who practice this, however, must make frequent revisions in the list, for they learn that God answers prayer.

5. *Thanksgiving*. Thanksgiving differs from adoration in that, while the latter praises God for what He is, the former thanks Him for what He has done. No prayer should be conducted without a time of thanksgiving. He who recognizes daily the countless blessings of God will find it hard to be critical or complaining. Thanksgiving, he will discover, ministers to the health of his own soul, and he is likely to learn the priceless lesson that when prayer is going poorly it is always profitable to turn to thanksgiving.

These five elements of prayer may seem very complicated for the working person who must conduct his devotions in a half-hour period each morning. Such is not the case, however. Once he has them clearly in mind, the Christian may move readily from one to another, stopping longer on some than others. But in following them, he will find his prayer life becoming orderly and more meaningful.

The Church in Your Life

The third means of grace, Christian fellowship, brings us to the subject of the church and its services of worship. The original language of the New Testament has two words for the church. The word *kuriakou* means simply "of the Lord," and from this, the English word, church, derives. The word *ecclesia*, on the other hand, means "called out." It was used to denote a group of people called out to meet in a certain place: hence, an assembly or a congregation. The idea of being called out from the world has also been attached to the word when the Christian church has been in mind.

In any event, the Church is a society of the redeemed, and the moment one is converted he is a member of this society. However, he should be quick to acknowledge his membership in the invisible Church by uniting with the visible church. Free Methodism sees clearly that faithful association with other Christians is essential to spiritual development. We must belong to grow.

We should turn our attention, because of this, to some practical instructions on how to get the most from the worship services of the church.

How to Profit from the Services of the Church

1. *Form the habit of regular attendance.*

We tend to reduce the important things in life to the level of habit, and it is well we do. How unmanageable life would become if it were not for the good habits we form. For example, imagine our confusion if each day we decided afresh whether to wash our faces, brush our teeth, comb our hair, or attend to the other numberless details that go into a day's living.

By reducing such practices to habit we make sure that the important things are not left out of our living, and we also form life into a meaningful pattern. Certainly, the Christian will put church attendance into the category of those habits that give his life meaning. Nothing good can result from having to make a new decision every time public worship hour draws near. Sunday school and morning worship, the evening evangelistic service, midweek prayer meeting--especially prayer meeting--are services which will become a regular part of the weekly routine for earnest Christians. Regularity in attendance will only come, however, from firm resolution! Discipleship requires discipline at this point.

2. *Form the habit of arriving early for services.*

A ten-minute period of meditation before any service will prepare the heart for communion with God. Haste and lateness (unavoidable on the rarest occasion) make worship difficult if not impossible.

Once I had to transport a guest from a campground to speak to my Sunday evening congregation. I realized the closeness of my schedule and so arranged with my song leader to begin the service at the appointed time in case I was late.

After making every minute count, we still arrived five minutes late. The service was in progress. I rushed to take my place on the platform and join in the spirit of the singing. But it was not possible. I discovered that the rush and lateness had robbed me of the impulse to worship. I felt throughout the service like a stranger who didn't belong.

Habitual lateness will spoil services for any layperson. But in addition, it will indicate that he does not feel responsible for the quality of the worship life of his church. And it will show that, in his heart, he is not deeply involved, coming to church more as a casual spectator than as an earnest participant. All this can be avoided only by persevering until the habit of arriving early enough for meditation is clearly formed.

3. *Choose wisely where you will sit for worship.*

Back seats are inadvisable, especially for young people, because the temptation to irreverence is especially high there. The choice to sit with wrong companions in a church service also puts the worshiper under special temptation. One must plan in advance not to sit "in the seat of the scornful."

Young Christians who are trying to form good habits of

worship will not look upon this as needless counsel. They will want to sit where they will themselves derive the greatest benefit from a service and where they will not be tempted to irreverence, spoiling the service for others around them.

4. *Worship throughout the service.*

Those who sit indifferently in a service, waiting until something touches them, overlook the very important fact that worship involves an act of the will. The informed Christian will come to service with the fixed purpose of worshiping. As he comes, he will be aware that he is to be in the presence of the Eternal God and that as he worships Him, he may expect to be made conscious of the nearness of the living Christ. All this, because even before he arrives, his will is set to worship.

Join in the hymns, singing thoughtfully and fervently. (Methodism at its best has always been characterized by fervent congregational singing.) Participate in prayer. Enter into the reading of the Scriptures by joining heartily in the responsive reading or by following along in your own Bible as a passage is read publicly. Listen to the sermon with openness. Show your hunger in your listening. Remember, you do not attend service so much to evaluate as to be evaluated.

5. *Regard yourself as a member of the welcoming committee.*

Every church member, however new in his relationship, should feel it his duty to greet visitors. (We never use the word "strangers" in our congregations.) Our churches will never be outstanding for their lofty architecture or their elaborate ritual, but we want them to be known by their warmth and friendliness. Visitors are touched by the outreach of love shown in a warm welcome. Every member should therefore feel responsible to express this warmth to those who visit in the services.

6. *Be sure to join the big four.*

The individual who attends church only one hour a week may be just one hour a week from being a thoroughly secular person. The third division of the historic General Rules on which Methodism came to maturity stressed the necessity for different kinds of Christian fellowship. Our churches have tended to develop their programs around what might be called the "big-four services." These are Sunday morning and evening services, the

Sunday school and the midweek prayer service.

Usually, in the Sunday morning service, the accent is on worship. This is the hour when the congregation corporately lifts its eyes Godward in "wonder, love, and praise." Worship is absolutely necessary to soul health. We must have times when as a people we ponder the majesty and love of the Almighty. Failing this, we will find ourselves suffering from a lost sense of perspective in life.

The Sunday evening service has traditionally been the outreach service of the week. It does not attract the unsaved as it did a few decades ago. This has led some congregations to experiment with films, dialogue, discussions, and so forth. The churches with the most vital and attractive Sunday evening services are still those that emphasize the authority of the Scriptures in preaching and teaching.

The measure of a congregation's power is in its prayer meeting. Many pastors strive to make this the most inspiring service of the week. This is done by a continuing Bible study and the division of the congregation into prayer cells, numbering from six to eight, for the prayer period. This has proved immeasurably valuable wherever it has been tried. After Bible study, these prayer cells congregate separately in Sunday school rooms or in other suitable places and pray together informally. In this way, a sympathetic atmosphere is created, and the timid can be more easily encouraged to learn to pray in public. Needs too can be shared before prayer begins.

Church leaders everywhere are beginning to realize the growth potential of the Sunday school. As one recent study reported, effective Christian education is the most powerful single influence in developing mature faith. In Sunday school people of all ages learn what the Bible says and are challenged to walk as Jesus walked. They are led in discovering that more than a set of teachings, faith is a way of living. Sunday school classes are the place where people form spiritually supportive relationships, are encouraged to ask the questions that disturb them most, and are motivated to serve others through acts of love, justice, and social ministry.

These are the big-four services to which every Christian

should be faithful. Each is necessary for well-rounded Christian development. Corporate worship keeps a congregation's eyes fixed on the true center of the universe, the eternal God. In the evening service, joyful singing, spontaneous testimonies, and whatever else may enhance the gospel unite the congregation in a corporate celebration of the good news of redemption in Christ. The midweek prayer service stands behind both these services, nurturing Christians in the faith and uniting them in intercession for spiritual needs at home and abroad. The Sunday school's ministry involves winning people to Christ, establishing them in the faith, and training them in turn to minister to others. All four are indispensable.

7. *Be a practicing Christian.*

When you leave a service, do so with the fixed purpose of assimilating into your daily living the truth you have heard. Don't hesitate to jot down notes if this enables you to receive the Word with greater alertness. Plan for a period of meditation as soon after the meeting as possible. Try to put into practice the lessons you have learned. In so doing, you will be following the counsel of James who said, "Be doers of the word, and not hearers only" (James 1:22, RSV).

The Sacrament of the Lord's Supper

The first three means of grace are the Bible, prayer, and Christian fellowship. To these we now add a fourth, the Lord's Supper.

Our church seeks to give this Sacrament its scriptural place in the local congregation. It is nowhere made necessary to salvation, since one is saved by grace through faith. At the same time, however, participation in this ordinance is in response to a command of our Lord (1 Corinthians 11:24-26). Therefore, failure to observe this Sacrament involves disobedience.

Our church does not hold the view of the Roman Catholic Church that the elements are transformed into the *actual* body and blood of Christ in the priest's performance of the Mass. Nor do we hold the Lutheran view that the body and blood of Christ are present with the elements as they are taken. For us, the Sacrament is a remembrance of Calvary, but it is more; it is a means of grace. That is, we believe that as we obediently follow the commandment of our Lord in partaking of the ordinance, we feed on them in our hearts by faith.

Our *Book of Discipline* states that this Sacrament must be observed at least once in three months.

It is an old Methodist custom to have the communicants come forward to receive the elements at the altar rail, and this custom has much to be said in its favor. For one thing, it symbolizes the idea of coming to the Lord's table. For another, it calls for an open avowal of faith which is not so necessary when the elements are served in the pews. If the communicants are carefully informed of the meaning of what they are doing, and if they are then invited to come forward to the table of the Lord, the likelihood that any will partake of the elements unworthily is somewhat reduced. As well, many have testified that to come forward seems to increase the spiritual meaning of the Sacrament.

When this practice has proved overly time-consuming for larger congregations, the problem has sometimes been solved by making the Communion the major part of the service. In such cases, the minister may give a Communion meditation in place of his regular sermon, and the rest of the service time is then available for the reverent observance of the Sacrament of the Lord's Supper. Thus, haste is not necessary.

Such a procedure does not minimize the central place of preaching in our services. It puts the minister under even greater obligation to prepare a shorter message which will speak to his people, and it does recognize the great value of this Sacrament which is observed in direct obedience to our Lord's command.

A Closing Word

Someone has aptly referred to our generation as the cut-flower generation. Cut flowers are rootless and, however beautiful, their very existence is threatened by the fact that they have no roots. Rootlessness is the Achilles heel of secularism. We Christians can be so enamored with the cosmetic beauty of our cut-flower peers that we drift toward the same sort of rootlessness. Unless, that is, we take seriously the means of grace, using them faithfully to send our roots ever deeper into the eternal God in whom "we live and move and have our being."

For Review:
1. What are the four means of grace discussed in this chapter?

2. State the three counsels one should follow in making the Bible a meaningful part of his life.

3. Restate the three directions for using the Bible.

4. List four different ways the Christian may engage in prayer.

5. What are the five elements of a well-rounded prayer?

6. Restate the suggestions one should follow to profit from the services of the church.

For Further Reading:
Murray, Andrew. *With Christ in the School of Prayer*. Westwood, New Jersey: Fleming H. Revell Company.

Parsons, Elmer E. *Living the Holy Life Today*. Indianapolis, Indiana: Light and Life Press, 1990.

Van Valin, Clyde E. *Transforming Grace*. Indianapolis, Indiana: Light and Life Press, 1990.

For further thought:
What steps could your church take to deepen the devotional life of its members?

What are the major foes to engaging in the practices that nurture? How do these touch your life?

CHAPTER NINE

However we see ourselves in relationship to the local church, we all have a common standard by which to measure ourselves. If our tendency is to love the church in the abstract more than in the concrete, we have the example of Jesus to consider. "Christ loved the church and gave himself up for her" (Ephesians 5:25). This was the church at Ephesus, at Corinth, at Sardis. It is the church down on your corner or across town--the church not yet fully cleansed of spots and wrinkles. His was a sacrificial love toward the church. Can we be aloof when He was involved?

The Church Where You Live

A man who wanted to be known for his great love for children one day poured a new driveway. The little four-year-old next door promptly left her footprints across its full width. Disgusted, he stormed to her mother to complain.

Her mother listened through the screen door and then said coolly, "I thought you were the man who had a great fondness for children." "I am," he replied, "but I like children in the abstract, not in the concrete."

When it comes to the church, some of us are like that man. We find it easier to love the church in the abstract than in the concrete.

The church's splendor in New Testament times, its achievements in past ages, its successes in other parts of the world--these win our outspoken admiration. But the church that meets down on the corner is a different matter. It's near at hand and under our close inspection it seems flawed. We come up with numerous reasons for loving it with reservation or withholding our love completely.

The Church in the Concrete

A Christian humorist of an earlier decade used to write about "Saint John's by the Gas Station"--a congregation bearing an ancient Christian's name but meeting in a modern and earthy setting. This chapter is about that sort of church. It may meet down on the corner (or out on the edge of town or in an inner city storefront building or on the fringe of a new housing development). Actually, it's the Free Methodist church you attend.

But before we move to the subject, we must look for a few moments at the word "church" itself. It's a word used in many different ways, and we can get confused if we don't pay some attention to this fact. We refer to the building where we meet as "our church." The people with whom we worship are also "our church." No less accurately do we call the Free Methodist denomination "our church."

This sort of complexity has been noted by theologians. One of them organizes the complexity this way: The church "is both divine and human, spiritual and material, invisible and visible, catholic and local, triumphant and militant, possessing continuity and vitality." Any phenomenon in history having all these characteristics must be discussed with deliberation.

Take just one of the descriptive pairs: The church is both catholic (universal) and local. That is, it encompasses all true believers in Jesus Christ throughout the world while at the same time manifesting itself in companies of believers who meet in designated localities. Neither aspect of this twofold reality cancels out the other. Both are true at the same time.

Furthermore, a local church is not merely a fragment of the universal church, in the way a splinter is part of a log. In a local assembly, the whole of the church is manifested. For this reason it is more accurate to say the church in Corinth than the Corinthian Church.

Must Christians be together to be the church? When a local congregation of Christians disperses, the church does not go out of existence. The gathered church becomes the scattered church. Such are the wonders of the church of Christ!

When we consider a local Free Methodist church, therefore, we are not merely looking at a sociological phenomenon, even though sociological factors do affect the complexion of any body. More profoundly, we are looking at one manifestation of the fulfillment of God's purpose in the world. God has always had a people. His people congregate in companies, as concrete expressions of the reality of the church universal. They function in a sense as stations of the catholic church.

It is this aspect of the church we take up now, giving special attention to the purpose and leadership of a local Free Methodist church.

What Is the Church For?

In their early years, children learn about their environment rapidly because of the way in which they ask their questions. Show a four-year-old a wheelbarrow for the first time and he is likely to ask, "What is it for?" (As adults, we might be more inclined to ask, "What is it?") The child seems to know intuitively that if you know the purpose of something you will come to understand it faster than if you simply get its name or description. Knowing its purpose, in fact, leads to an understanding of its nature.

We can ask of our local church, "What is it?" The answers will come in rapid succession: The church is a community of Christian believers. The church is the body of Christ in the world. The church is a messianic community. The church is a colony of heaven. The church is a temple of the Spirit. The church is . . .

But not until we ask "What is the church for?" do we begin to understand with clarity what it is.

1. *The church is for worship.*

We Christians have come into covenant with a God who has made himself known. We say He is self-revealed. "For since the creation of the world God's invisible qualities--his eternal power and divine nature--have been clearly seen, being understood from what has been made" (Romans 1:20). That is, God has made something of himself known in the created universe. In Jesus Christ, He has made himself fully known. Jesus shines with "the brightness of God's glory and is the exact likeness of God's own being" (Hebrews 1:3, TEV).

God's self-revelation tells us what we could not otherwise know: He is absolutely holy, yet the friend of sinners; He is transcendent, yet willing to take up residence in His created world; He is eternal but with us in every moment of our lives. Like the psalmist, we confess, "Such knowledge is too wonderful for me, too lofty for me to attain" (Psalm 139:6).

We may not be able to attain such knowledge, but it moves us to respond. Worship is the natural response--wonder, adoration, fear, thanksgiving. The God we worship is at the same time incomprehensible and fully revealed in Jesus. Christian worship is human response to that revelation, the fundamental activity of the church.

When a local church perceives this, it organizes all its activities around worship. There is public worship and private worship, formal worship and informal worship, corporate worship and family worship. The local church worships in song and in prayer; its people worship at table and at bedside. Committees meet to worship and work. Teams meet to worship and serve. An authentic local church worships God in spirit and in reality; that's what it is for.

2. *The church is for fellowship.*

The symbol for fellowship in the church is not the testimony service nor the social evening nor even the home Bible study. It is the Lord's Supper.

Christian fellowship is the sharing of a common life in Christ. Fellowship is the way people relate to one another when they discover that God looks upon them in grace and mercy. Fellowship has many elements--concern, mutual rejoicing, loving honesty, forgiveness, the sharing of burdens, laughter. But all elements are especially charged with Calvary love. That is what distinguishes Christian fellowship from mere socializing.

Fellowship sets up a climate in which aspiring Christians are able to know one another and be known. As it develops, Christians may accept the full range of their own humanity, including both the wonder of God's creation in them and the flaws caused by sin. It opens the way for growth in the acknowledgment of weaknesses and the appropriation of grace. Fellowship is life lived in Christ and in Christ's church.

There's a vacuum in modern life which the church is equipped to fill. In every community, people languish for something akin to fellowship. In honest moments they complain fretfully that jobs are boring, social relationships are shallow, and family life is precarious. Some have experienced that secular alternatives to Christian fellowship are always inadequate and sometimes damaging.

The church has the resources in Christ to meet the world's great deficiency. It is in Christian fellowship.

3. *The church is for ministry.*

We often reserve the word "minister" for a select person appointed to give leadership to a congregation on a professional and full-time basis. This is good in that it suggests the nature of this leader's role: He is servant, not ruler; and by the church he is placed in a position of responsibility, not privilege. The title is apt.

But to consider such a person as the sole minister in a local church is to deviate seriously from the New Testament. In a wider and less specialized sense, the work of the whole church is ministry. The gifts the resurrected Christ bestowed upon the church--apostles, prophets, evangelists, and others--were given to equip the saints "for the work of ministry" (Ephesians 4:12, RSV).

Jesus himself came to be a minister and in doing so to establish a standard for all His followers. "The Son of man came not to be ministered unto, but to minister . . ." (Mark 10:45, KJV). His life was a demonstration of servanthood. He healed the infirm, restored the demented, and, in a great symbolic act, washed the feet of His own disciples. The servanthood of Jesus was not lost on His immediate followers. In response, Paul regularly referred to himself as the servant of Jesus Christ.

Therefore, the local church in full health is marked by ministry. Its organizational structure provides for officers whose first duty is to serve the needy. There are deaconesses and stewards who minister in the church and community. As the gospel awakens generous and compassionate impulses, ministry becomes spontaneous as well as assigned. The church shows itself to be a caring institution.

This ministry of the local church is first of all toward itself. The local church is a fellowship of people who assume responsibility for one another. The Apostle Paul highlighted this primary responsibility when he said, "So then, as we have opportunity, let us do good to all men, and especially to those who are of the household of faith" (Galatians 6:10, RSV).

But the servanthood of the local church does not end with ministry to its own. Wherever the church has gone around the world, it has demonstrated ministry in a wide variety of ways. Abandoned children have been cared for, the infirm have been comforted and helped. Hostels, orphanages, hospitals, schools, rest homes are found wherever the church is.

As the sense of servanthood deepens, some Christians become ministers to their state or country, making their voice heard on social issues and entering the political arena to speak for righteousness.

4. *The church is for evangelism.*

Evangelism is not a fad for over-ardent churches nor an

elective for seasonal emphases. Nor is it a method for the swelling of statistics. It may be attended by spiritual ardor and practiced during special seasons, and it is sure to bring growth to a church. But at heart, evangelism is a spirit-implanted desire to spread the good news that Jesus Christ is the world's Savior, to invite people to receive him by personal faith and become members of His church.

Evangelism is an integral activity of the church because of Jesus. Just before His ascension, He said to His followers, the nucleus of the Christian church, "All authority in heaven and on earth has been given to me. Therefore go and make disciples of all nations, baptizing them in the name of the Father and of the Son and of the Holy Spirit, and teaching them to obey everything I have commanded you. And surely I am with you always, to the very end of the age" (Matthew 28:18-20).

This Great Commission is recorded five times in the New Testament. The first Christian leaders took it literally; and before one generation had passed, the gospel had been propagated and the church planted throughout the Roman world.

Local churches may lose this concern, becoming institutions more than movements. They may even continue to exist in apparent health, living on the spiritual nutrients supplied by a previous generation. But close inspection will reveal otherwise. The church is for evangelism and it cannot be robust and self-fulfilled unless it is fulfilling God's purpose for its existence.

Some Words of Clarification

The church is indeed for worship, fellowship, ministry, and evangelism but it does not exist for these ends in a mechanical way. That is, it does not gather on one occasion for fellowship exclusively and on another for ministry. The four purposes of the church are separated only to aid understanding. The church is an organism, and the four purposes may be fulfilled at one and the same time, or one may flow naturally into another.

For example, a congregation may gather for worship and in the experience come to a deep level of fellowship, while if it is assembled for fellowship exclusively it may disperse disappointed. Few things are harder to sustain than fellowship when sought as an end in itself. But let Christians gather for ministry--and fellowship will result. Let two Christians be involved in evangelism--and before their assignment is completed they may experience a joy that moves them to worship.

We must be clear about this interlocking nature of the purposes of the church. We must be clear also about the place of education in its corporate life.

You may have noticed that education was not included as one of the purposes of the church. It was not left out because it is unimportant. It is, in fact, one of the most important activities of the local church, and every healthy church gives it a large place in its corporate life. The reason it was not included in the purposes of the church is that education is not an end in itself. It is a handmaiden, teaching Christians to worship, fellowship, serve, and evangelize.

When this is perceived in a local church, the teaching task is always looking beyond itself, and educational ministries are characterized by clear objectives. If it becomes an end in itself, teaching involves largely an exchange of information, a swapping of religious opinions, or the debating of fine points of doctrine. Let Christian education fuel the purposes of the church, and information becomes information to some end, while learning is marked by spiritual vitality.

Who Are The Church's Leaders?

We must now consider the leaders of a local Free Methodist church. No organization can be stronger than its leaders, nor can it function with a high sense of morale without strong and sensitive leadership.

This does not diminish the importance of the Holy Spirit in directing the life of a local church. It only recognizes that the Holy Spirit works through humans, and His work may be aided or limited by them.

The Minister

What shall we call the appointed leader of a local Free Methodist Church--preacher? reverend? pastor? brother? Preacher is inadequate, because he does more than preach. Reverend is more formal and takes some doing to use correctly (The Reverend Mr. So and So). Pastor is rising in popularity, and as a title of address it has a combination of respect and warmth. Brother is always appropriate in a Christian community--unless the leader is a sister.

Our *Book of Discipline* most commonly refers to the leader as a minister, a person who is at the same time a servant of the Lord and a servant of the congregation.

In the Free Methodist Church, there are two levels of ordination for a minister. After meeting established requirements of education and experience, he is first ordained deacon. This office traces back to the deacons set apart for ministry by the early church (Acts 6). The deacon is to fill a servant role (as the word denotes), giving special care to the pastoral needs of a congregation and sometimes working under an elder. At his ordination, he is reminded that Stephen, the first martyr, was a deacon.

The second level of ordination is to the office of elder, the highest ordination the Free Methodist Church recognizes. The elder therefore may perform all the functions of ministry, may serve on the conference stationing committee, and may be elected to the superintendency or bishopric.

The Free Methodist minister, either deacon or elder, is a member of an annual conference, one of thirty-six into which the church in North America is divided. His conference guides him, ordains him, and appoints him to his place of service. Each year the church he serves is given opportunity to vote on his return. This along with the report of his delegate(s), the record of his ministry, and other factors are taken into account in his further appointment. Thus the minister is answerable to his annual conference and his appointment is made with sensitive attention to the needs of everyone concerned.

Gifted ministers, like exceptional leaders in all fields, are not numerous. A church that has a good ministerial leader, therefore, should cooperate with him as fully as it can. This includes making his work as fulfilling for him as possible. Most ministers work for challenge, not for dollars. They should not be unnecessarily deprived of adequate support because of this, but they should be given encouragement in exercising their leadership. Effective ministers are never satisfied to carry on with a bare maintenance program.

If a church does not have an exceptional minister, or if its minister is young and inexperienced, it should be concerned to help him grow. It is true that great ministers make great churches, but great churches make great ministers, too. Churches differ widely in their ability to draw the best out of their leader. By its attitudes, a church may make or break its minister.

Here are some things you, as a new member, can do to help your minister be the best leader possible.

1. *Love Him*

You need not be fawning or sentimental to your leader, but you can project goodwill toward him. Thank him specifically for his work ("Your message on the Christian hope cleared up some things for me"). Drop him a note of appreciation in the mail during special seasons. Ministers, like other humans, grow when they are loved.

2. *Work with him.*

Every church has at least one person who feels compelled to resist leadership either passively or actively. Don't let yourself be that person. You do not have to agree with every plan or project your minister proposes. But whenever you can, work with him, not against him. He'll feel your support.

3. *Encourage members of the official board to make opportunities for him to grow.*

Ministers need experiences to keep them growing. They should attend at least two conferences or seminars a year. They need good books for their minds and proper vacations for renewal. Every minister should be provided with adequate working space for study as well as a commodious room in which to receive those who come seeking help.

4. *Register complaints ethically.*

You are not expected to agree with everything your minister does. Some things (he does or doesn't do) may offend you deeply. Ministers like all other humans, fall short at times. When this happens our skill and grace will be tested. Whenever possible, speak to him directly in love. If the issue you wish to raise is serious and cannot be brought to him it should be shared with the pastor's cabinet or even the conference superintendent. This gives opportunity for you to check your impressions against theirs.

At no time should complaints be registered to persons not directly involved. You will have a hard time convincing yourself you have gone to them out of good motives when you have not taken your complaints to those who can deal with them. Evil speaking is a disruptive influence in troubled congregations. It's unethical and sinful.

5. *Support him with your means.*

The Apostle Paul wrote, "People under instruction should always contribute something to the support of the man who is instructing them" (Galatians 6:8, *Jerusalem Bible*). When you place a regular offering in the offering plate, part of your gift goes to the support of your minister. You'll be surprised how your love and loyalty deepen as you add your financial support to that of other members of the church.

The Lay Leaders

The minister may be the appointed and focal leader of your church but he is by no means its only leader. Every thriving church is marked by a growing number of lay leaders as well.

We tend to use the word "layman" or "layperson" with an air of apology. For example, when we ask a specialist for information or advice, we demur, saying, "I'm only a layperson." It's as if we are saying, "I'm not very smart." The word layperson has taken on a self-belittling tone.

Actually, "layperson" and "laity" come from an ancient Greek root which means simply "the people." Used of the church in its broadest sense, it means all the people. There is nothing downgrading about it. In this wider sense, we are all laypersons.

But as clergy became more sharply distinguished from laypersons in the centuries after Christ, they also were elevated above laypersons. This led to the notion that laypersons are an inferior order of Christians. There is no biblical warrant for such an idea.

The Free Methodist Church was organized on August 23,

1860, by a convention of eighty laypersons and fifteen ministers. One of the founding principles of her government was that in all Annual and General Conference plenary sessions and committee structures, there should be an equal representation of laypersons and ministers. This is a distinctive feature of the Free Methodist Church. For example, if an annual conference is composed of one hundred delegates from churches, approximately fifty will be laypersons and fifty will be ministers.

The church goes poorly where lay leadership is not actively cultivated. In fact, a one-man church is no church at all. God does not bestow His gifts exclusively on ministers for the good of passive laypersons; He bestows gifts on all "the people" so that they can minister to one another, each making a special contribution to all.

I have warm memories of serving a church in which there were 156 laypersons elected to positions of leadership. They were teachers, directors, committeepersons, stewards, trustees, visitors, supervisors, and so on. It was a sheer joy to see this nucleus of Christians learn their jobs and bring their particular abilities to bear on the tasks assigned them. Needless to say, morale in the church was generally high.

As a local Free Methodist church puts its people to work for the Lord, some begin to manifest greater leadership skills than others. It is then the task of minister and nominating committee to recommend those leaders for key positions in such a way as to distribute their talents for leadership evenly throughout the church. To use a mechanical image, they become the spark plugs to fire the life of the church for worship, fellowship, ministry, and evangelism.

Tips for Lay Leaders

If you are a layperson with an emerging gift for leadership, here are some suggestions. Follow them--and the spiritual health of the congregation, as well as your own, will be enhanced.

1. *Let the church match your abilities to tasks.*

The nominating committee will want to place you where you can do the most good for the Lord. They will likely ask you about your preferences as well as surveying the church's needs. After they have evaluated your present level of ability their decision will be submitted to the official board or even the annual society meeting for a vote. The objective will be to disperse emerging leaders throughout the church for ministry.

You may be apprehensive about the judgment of a committee. Unless you have a compelling reason to do otherwise, however, trust the Lord to guide His people for His glory and your good.

One warmhearted woman was assigned to teach a high school class. Class order nose-dived. She made herself amenable to Sunday school leaders, and they carefully and deliberately reassigned her (following procedures) to teach a class of nine-year-old girls. She was an instant success and the class began to thrive. If she had not trusted herself to the judgment of the church, in spite of an earlier error, her leadership skill would not likely have been discovered.

2. *Learn how the church organization works, and work as deftly as possible within it.*

Wherever two or more people set about to do a common task, whether it be to prepare a picnic lunch or to wash a car, organization emerges. The alternative is confusion at best and chaos at worst. Some distrust organization, considering it unwieldy and impersonal. It need not be. The most prominent leaders of Bible times were careful organizers--Moses, Nehemiah, David, Solomon, the Apostle Paul and, above all, Jesus. If you take pains to learn how organization works within your church and then follow its lines, you can use it to the glory of God.

Some argue that the method of government used by Free Methodist churches is inferior to methods used in other communions. As a matter of fact, it has been shown that there are thriving churches using all different forms of government. Other churches on the same form are doing poorly. What matters is that you understand and follow the procedures by which your church is governed.

This is especially important when it comes to relationships between ministerial and lay leaders. To work as a team, respect must go both ways, and proper procedures must be followed. Carnality has a heyday in poorly governed churches.

3. *Accept opportunities for service nearest at hand.*

It's easy to stand back waiting for the big challenge, but the Christian who accepts the little challenge with zest is most likely to handle the big one well. Jesus said, "Whoever can be trusted with very little can also be trusted with much" (Luke 16:10). Your leadership skills will grow only as they are exercised on the nearest and sometimes smallest assignment.

4. *Cultivate the spirit of faithfulness.*

When the Apostle Paul listed the elements making up the fruit of the Spirit, love headed the list (Galatians 5: 22, 23). In the Christian life, everything begins with God's kind of love. But a distance down the list comes the grace of faithfulness. In the growing Christian, faith gives rise to faithfulness; the Christ-trusting person becomes the trustworthy person. A leader not only has a charisma about him, but he can be counted on as well.

Practice the art of loyalty to your minister. He is the officially appointed leader of the local church and loyalty to him helps to give cohesion to the body. Sometimes as lay leaders develop, in subtle ways they become competitive with the minister. This is both shortsighted and immature and will give the minister a sense of dissonance, if not of diminished worth. The mature stance for lay leaders is one of solid loyalty to their minister, giving a ground for the hammering out of plans and the testing of ideas in mutually respectful dialogue.

The local church with a spiritual and competent ministerial leader and a growing number of lay leaders will reflect this by the enrichment of congregational life and the growth of the body. God's hand upon His people will be evident in the way they are led in worship, fellowship, ministry, and evangelism.

Lay Leaders on the Way to Full-time Ministry

Where do ministers come from in the Free Methodist Church? We know they are a class of persons specially called by God. We know that the annual conference has a Board of Ministerial Education and Guidance that processes and directs them and that normally they get their formal training through college and seminary. But how and where does the process all get started?

It should begin in the local church. Every church is charged with the responsibility of recognizing persons who give evidence of a special call to full-time ministry. Such persons are distinguished by both gifts and graces. The church may be God's instrument in helping a candidate to hear and recognize a call.

In fact, this assignment is so important that responsibility for carrying it out is lodged with the official board of the church. If, in the judgment of the board, a person shows signs of having both gifts and graces for ministry, the board has authority to approve this person as a local ministerial candidate.

In the earlier days of Methodism in England, local preachers were the "heroes" of the movement. They were laymen who were licensed and assigned to care for the societies. The same was so in the colonies less than half a century later. The preachers--fewer than one hundred in number--who gathered in Baltimore in 1784 to organize the Methodist Episcopal Church, were local preachers, including the noted Francis Asbury.

At that time, the issuing of a local preacher's license became the first step toward ordination, first to deacon's orders and then to elder's orders. Increasing numbers moved on from the initial license to full ordination.

Nowadays, the title has been changed from local preacher to local ministerial candidate. Qualifications include full membership in the Free Methodist Church, a declared call to preach, and successful completions of a specified study course monitored by the pastor. After a period of careful supervision at the local level, the ministerial candidate may be recommended to the conference to become a conference ministerial candidate. The conference board of ministerial education and guidance reviews the candidate's qualifications, and if the requirements have been fulfilled acts affirmatively on the recommendation. From that point on this board assumes responsibility for the supervision of the candidate with regard both to education and training.

There are some church members who desire to be used in ministry but do not feel called to a full-time vocation. To accommodate this desire and enlarge the ministry of the church, such a person may be granted a lay minister's license. Such persons serve alongside the pastoral staff at the local level of the church.

Obviously, the church recognizes more than two distinct

classes--ministers and lay persons. There are some on the way to becoming ministers or wishing, by means of directed studies and licensing, to equip themselves to serve the Lord in a special way at the local level.

How Does a Local Free Methodist Church Get Things Done?

You will recall that every Free Methodist church exists for a fourfold purpose. How does it go about seeing this fourfold purpose fulfilled?

The society--operating within broad guidelines set forth in the *Book of Discipline*--decides what is to be done locally. But the society cannot be called together every time a decision is to be made or a project launched. It therefore elects officers, committees, and boards who together constitute an official board. The personnel of this board, as well as its rights and responsibilities, are outlined in the *Book of Discipline* (¶A/402). Committees of the board attend to specific tasks, and the unity of the government of the church is achieved as these committees remain answerable to the board and the board to the society.

All sorts of jokes are made these days about the structures that give direction to the life of a local church. The meeting of the board is sometimes referred to as the meeting of the "bored." Committees are described as bodies that keep minutes and waste hours. The charges are too often true.

A seminary professor in California, for example, asked lay leaders from several churches the following question: "Since serving on a church board, do you feel that your spiritual life has improved or declined?" More than 80 percent reported that their spiritual life had declined. Local churches in all too many cases must have lost their sense of purpose. In spite of this response, certain facts have to be faced.

First, no local church can fulfill its ministry unless its energies are governed. Poorly governed, it may survive as an ingrown sociological group for a long while. But if it is to thrive as a company of God's people in its community it must be organized to do so. Second, there are ways in which a church can be directed so as to make its government a source of blessing.

Here are ten marks of a well-managed church:

1. *The church operates according to clearly defined purposes.*

Early in this chapter, four purposes were enunciated. These could be fittingly adopted by any Free Methodist church, but not without careful deliberation. Adopted simply because they had been recommended in a book, they would have little effect upon the life of the church. Every local church must ask searching questions about the reasons for its existence, praying and deliberating until poorly focused purposes become clearly focused. In a well-managed church, purposes are defined, adopted, and known to the membership. Known in this way, they energize the life and program of the whole congregation.

2. *The church has goals which are reviewed and revised periodically.*

A goal is distinguished by the fact that it can be measured and a time set for its completion. Purposes are not measurable. Even so, goals cannot be set until purposes are clear. For example, the purpose of a local church may be to cultivate the life of prayer. One goal may then be to develop a midweek prayer and Bible study hour that reaches an attendance equal to half the number of its members. This goal is measurable. In another case, if a church's purpose is to make worship a part of every activity, it may then set as a goal the establishment of a family altar in the homes of all its members. Each church must do the detailed and painstaking work of establishing realistic goals in accordance with stated purposes.

3. *The official board meets regularly.*

The more spiritually vigorous and purposeful a church, the more important it is that its board meet regularly. Some boards meet a certain night once a month. Others meet following the midweek service every first midweek meeting of the month. Whatever the time of meeting, the well-governed church places it on a regular schedule. Members are notified, and in some cases major items to be dealt with are known in advance.

4. *In a well-governed church, workers know their tasks.*

When the services of workers are solicited by a nominating committee or, in key cases, by the pastor, the task is outlined to them. This is usually followed by a written description of the task and an opportunity to ask clarifying questions. Nothing is more demoralizing to a church than to give people tasks that they don't understand or that don't seem important to them.

5. *Responsibility is wisely spread throughout the congregation.*

The nominating committee tries to avoid putting too much responsibility on too few people. In a well-governed church, major committees do not have an overlap of membership, and no one person is asked to do several important tasks. Such a dispersion of responsibility may not be achieved in one year, but it can be achieved.

6. *Key leaders are strategically assigned.*

People who show skill in rallying the energies of others and in fulfilling their tasks are never numerous. In a well-managed church, therefore, they are carefully dispersed. For example, the nominating committee sees to it that two persons who are gifted to lead do not sit on the same committee while another committee is left without anyone so gifted. This kind of dispersion is constantly attempted as a church grows.

7. *In a well-governed church, the worship of God is a part of every activity.*

For example, a committee seeks the will of God as ardently as a Sunday morning worship congregation. The manner may be different but the object is the same. It is not unusual for a board to turn its interests to prayer as a special problem comes before it. Whatever cannot be hallowed by worship does not have a place in the life of a congregation. Churches cease to have boring board and committee meetings when they discover the spiritual dimension in everything they do.

8. *People not able to serve are replaced.*

Sometimes Christians do not serve in the position to which they are elected because the position has not been explained. They simply discover that they have a job. The fault in this case is with the leaders. But if a task has been explained and assigned and the person is unable to fulfill the assignment, with the greatest regard for everyone concerned, the position should be filled by someone able to serve. This raising of expectation always has a surprising effect upon a church. It lifts the morale of the whole body.

9. *Everyone is accountable.*

In a well-governed church, committees are accountable to the official board and the board is accountable to the society. In all this, the minister serves as a unifying person, a catalyst of the church's energies. If this principle of accountability is not practiced, groups in the church may get at cross purposes with each other and some may operate in demoralizing independence.

10. *A pastor's cabinet serves as a liaison between the pastor and the congregation.*

The cabinet, composed of key leaders of the church, is elected by the society. It regularly meets with the pastor, considering ideas for the life and growth of the church. It also communicates ideas from members of the congregation. The relationship between pastor and cabinet is ideal when there is enough trust to make talking possible and enough honesty to make two-way communication valuable. Misunderstandings can be averted in a church and new directions set when a pastor's cabinet functions well.

A Closing Word

The local church is the growing edge of the whole church enterprise in the world. It is also the growing edge of the denomination, one branch of the whole of God's people. Therefore, the leadership and government of that local station of Christ's church is crucial. In any local church, there are three kinds of leaders--risk-takers, caretakers, and undertakers.

The risk-taker is not merely a gambler. He carefully assesses a situation, seeing the new possibilities within it. In a wholesome way, he is visionary. His risks are calculated, and he derives blessing from helping his followers to see and share the risks--for Christ's sake.

The risks may have to do with new ministries, new approaches to evangelism, the planting of new churches, outreach into new communities, new ways of experiencing Christian fellowship, or new ways to make worship more meaningful to

God's people. You'll see all these concerns reflected in the vibrant church of New Testament times.

The risk-taker knows better than to lead his followers in an incessant confrontation with risk. Christians, too, are creatures of habit, and to have old habits constantly assailed is unsettling. In any healthy church there is a balance between continuity and innovation. Wise risk-takers see this. Theirs is the artistic task of appreciating all that is traditional while building on that foundation for growth.

The caretaker-type leader is more interested in maintenance. He thinks in terms of leaving things no worse than he found them. He is the faithful sort but cautious and unvisionary. Caretaker leaders are not nearly so stimulating to be around as risk-takers.

The problem so far as the church is concerned is that caretaker leaders too often pave the way for the undertaker. He, too, is a kind of leader, presiding with dignity over the affairs of death. Local churches too long on a caretaker regime will eventually be ready for the ministrations of the undertaker.

However we see ourselves in relationship to the local church, we all have a common standard by which to measure ourselves. If our tendency is to love the church in the abstract more than in the concrete, we have the example of Jesus to consider. "Christ loved the church and gave himself up for her" (Ephesians 5:25). This was the church at Ephesus, at Corinth, at Sardis. It is the church down on your corner or across town--the church not yet fully cleansed of spots and wrinkles. His was a sacrificial love toward the church. Can we be aloof when He was involved?

Wherever we locate ourselves in the leadership of a local church, whether high or low, we also have Christ's kind of leadership to follow. He counted not His life dear unto death. That was the supreme risk and it is continuing to bring forth large results around the world.

Being a mature church member involves wanting the best and giving the best at some local station of Christ's universal church.

For Review:
1. What are the four purposes of the local church?

2. State five things you can do to help your minister be the best leader possible.

3. List four suggestions for laymen who are emerging leaders.

4. Restate the ten marks of a well-managed church.

For Further Reading:

> *Book of Discipline*, Free Methodist Church, 1989. Indianapolis, Indiana: Light and Life Press. Chapter IV, "Official Bodies of the Church."

> The denominational magazine, *Light and Life*, as well as other denominational periodicals and handbooks.

For Further Thought:
Think of a recent church activity you attended, then identify in it the elements of worship, fellowship, ministry, and evangelism.

If you had your choice, what task would you choose for yourself in your church? Why would you choose this? What long-range plan would you follow if that task became yours?

CHAPTER TEN

There are 82,000 Free Methodists in North America, organized into 1,200 congregations, and the congregations are organized into 35 conferences. Abroad, there are another 170,000 Free Methodists in areas as widely separated as Japan and Paraguay, India and Ireland. There more than 250,000 souls are tied together formally by a common constitution, historically by a common heritage, and dynamically by common Christian commitments and goals.

To put it yet another way, the Free Methodist denomination is one branch of the universal church. It is not a large branch. There are some denominations in North America, for example, that number more than 10 million members. But a branch of a vine is a living, growing thing, and it is not so much by thickness of foliage as by fruitfulness.

The Church as Extended Family

Ed and Mildred Garvin were waiting at a bus stop in Manila, the Philippines, one warm day in the fall of 1974.

The Garvins had been in Manila less than two months, and in a city of four million, they still needed help to find their way around.

It was the Tuloy Crossing bus that the Garvins wanted to take. Did it or did it not stop where they waited? Not being sure, they asked a young Filipino woman who was standing at the stop.

She was instantly helpful. "That's the one I am taking," she said. "I'll take you with me."

Her name was Eden--Eden Liwag. Aboard the bus, Eden asked, "Where do you want to go?" When they gave her the name of the church-related institution, her interest quickened. "Is that your church?" she asked.

Mildred answered in the negative, explaining that they were of the Free Methodist Church. Eden responded with surprise, "Oh, that is my church! But I cannot find it here on the island of Luzon. It is sad that there is no Free Methodist Church in Manila."

The Garvins learned that back in 1960, in Butuan City several hundred miles to the south, Eden, then a child, had heard the gospel in a Free Methodist evangelistic crusade. Butuan City Free Methodist Church had provided the enthusiasm for the crusade, and Free Methodists from North America sent the preacher. Eden learned about Jesus Christ in that crusade and gave her heart to Him.

A few weeks later, while she was attending a Christian Youth Crusader's Camp, Free Methodist missionary Ray Streutker baptized her.

Eden's childhood passed rapidly. When she was old enough to get a job on her own, her mother sent her to Manila to attend a school for the training of beauticians. There was no Free Methodist church in Manila and the big city was distracting. She moved away from the Lord.

Before the bus ride ended, Eden told the Garvins: "I've not been in a Free Methodist church for years. I am so lonely for the

Lord. I am so lonely for my church."

Eden had married a nominal Catholic who did not want to go to church with her. The Garvins got her address, called on her, and met her husband, Pepito, a fine young television engineer.

When the Reverend Ray Streutker, mission superintendent who lived in Butuan City, came to Manila, the Garvins took him to meet the Liwags and to visit many other Free Methodists who had located in Manila. When the conference superintendent, the Reverend Managbanag, came, they introduced him around too.

Together, these leaders arranged for a meeting in a large United Methodist Church. Pepito and Eden Liwag and their little son Jonathan were among the first to attend.

The very next Saturday afternoon, Ed Garvin went to the Liwag home for a Bible study. Pepito and a carpenter he had hired were busily remodeling the apartment. But he dismissed the carpenter, came into the living room, took his Bible on his lap, and responded warmly, as Ed showed him that Jesus Christ had come to be his Savior.

Pepito and Eden were among the organizing members of the Free Methodist Church in Manila. This lone congregation began meeting in a United Methodist Church then in the Philippine Bible Society before settling down in 1976 in a large upstairs air-conditioned room of the Guzman School of Technology at the center of the city.

Did the work grow? Sixteen years later there were 14 Free Methodist churches in greater Manila. This included 10 fully organized churches and four preaching points on the way to becoming organized. The John Wesley Bible College was also established in 1983. In fact, enough churches have developed to allow the formation of an annual conference. This means there are now two conferences in the Philippines and the growth continues in both.

The original annual conference was on the island of Mindanao at the southern end of the Philippine archipelago. This too is a relatively young conference but already there are 107 local churches divided into five districts. Annual growth and membership in a recent year was 7.7 percent. The total membership of the southern conference is 10,349 which marks an actual increase of 742 members for the last year for which membership figures are available.

The story of the planting of the Free Methodist Church in Manila under the leadership of missionary Ray Streutker shows us another dimension of our Free Methodist communion. The congregation meeting upstairs in the school of technology was a local church--a particular station of the worldwide church of Jesus Christ. But it came into being through the deliberate energies of a denomination--the Free Methodist Church of North America. The combined efforts of the first annual conference of the Philippines with the North American Church led to the establishment of another conference in Quezon centering in Manila on the island of Luzon.

The object of this chapter is to acquaint you with the Free Methodist Church as your extended family. It is about the church you belong to and its varied ministries in the world.

The new conference on Luzon island in the Philippines is not the only significant development in recent years. In the 1980s alone, new fields have been opened in South America, one in Chile, one in Venezuela, and one in Ecuador. The field in Chile is growing very fast. Already there are more than 30 churches and preaching points. In March of 1990, the Commission on Missions voted to establish a mission district in the country of Bolivia as soon as funding is available.

All the while, the field in Central Africa continues to thrive with new work beginning in Kenya, Camaroon, and Nigeria. The countries of Burundi, Rwanda, and Zaire, the region where the Free Methodist church was first established in central Africa, are poor economically, but the church in these countries is the story of a modern Pentecost. In 1902, J.W. Haley, the first Canadian missionary sent by the Free Methodist Church, went to southern Africa. Later, under what he believed to be the Lord's leadership, he went into central Africa. The three fields--Burundi, Rwanda, and Zaire--have grown largely as a result of his labors. In these three countries alone, as of 1990, there were 112,000 Free Methodists, making this the largest concentration of Free Methodists in the world, exceeding even the number here in North America.

The Church in a Larger Perspective

The Manila story prompts us to take another look at the word "church." We learned earlier that the church is both local and universal. That is, it is a company of people who gather to worship and serve Christ in some specific locale, while at the same time it is all believers everywhere who worship and serve Christ.

Consider another classification, one not found in the theology texts. Think of the church as both racial and familial in the way humans are racial and familial. You, for example, a member of the human race within that race are a member of a particular family of humans--the McCartneys or Strabinskys or the Does. The McCartneys are humans linked to one another by common blood and we hope by common commitments and loyalties.

In a similar way, racially you may be a Christian and familially a Free Methodist. By your faith in Christ you are linked to all true believers everywhere--members of God's new race. But, because of providences which have touched your life --the place you grew up or the people who won you to Christ or the Christian college you attended or the pastor who reached you in a time of distress--you are a member of a family of people within that new race, the Free Methodists.

There are 82,000 Free Methodists in North America, organized into more than 1,200 congregations, and the congregations are organized into 35 conferences. Abroad, there are another 170,000 Free Methodists in areas as widely separated as Japan and Paraguay, India and Ireland. These more than 250,000 souls are tied together formally by a common constitution, historically by a common heritage, and dynamically by common Christian commitments and goals.

To put it yet another way, the Free Methodist denomination is one branch of the universal church. It is not a large branch. There are some denominations in North America, for example, that number more than 10 million members. But a branch of a vine is a living, growing thing, and it is not measured so much by thickness or foliage as by fruitfulness.

Since 1960, the Free Methodist Church of North America has been aggressively and daringly shifting responsible leadership to national leaders around the world. In 1960, the work in Japan and Egypt became General Conferences, with the right to elect their own bishops. In 1985, the Rwanda field became a full General Conference and Burundi a provisional General Conference. In 1989, India and Zaire became provisional General Conferences. In 1990, the Free Methodist Church in Canada was inaugurated as a General Conference.

In each of these cases, the policy has been to assist fields that have grown to maturity to assume more responsibility for their own leadership and development. All General Conferences are linked by a common constitution. A counsel of bishops brings the bishops from all these areas together periodically for consultation and planning.

The Free Methodist Church
Is an Evangelistic Body

Let me begin with a personal word: I was converted to Jesus Christ in March, 1942, in a little Free Methodist church in Estevan, Saskatchewan. I was sixteen years old.

It was a simple church in a small prairie community. Built soon after the turn of the century, the white clapboard-sided structure was heated by a floor furnace that released its warmth through a large register in the one aisle. The hymnbooks had words without music. The minister was his own songleader, though one of the more musical members usually "pitched the tune." Things weren't exactly sophisticated back then.

What I remember best, however, is that the people believed ardently. I felt it even before I could understand it. They believed in Jesus Christ as the world's only Savior. They believed in heaven and hell. It was their conviction that all men were sinners and God called everyone to repent and have faith in His Son. They were practitioners of holiness. They believed in love and demonstrated it, even to the offering of apologies when love failed. I saw this.

I remember too that the people loved me. No cold doctrinaire Christians, they patted me on the shoulder when I was small, enjoyed my Sunday school recitations, and told me of their prayers for my conversion as I grew through my early teens.

When I was converted, I responded to the love of Christ mediated through a devout mother and a supportive though unconverted father plus the community of a concerned church. The simple, straightforward doctrines I had heard from childhood prepared me to make a personal response to the call of Christ. As I remember, the congregation's concern for the salvation of sinners was evident and always present.

Evangelism involves ardent belief in Christian doctrines centering in God's love for sinners. It involves the conviction that sin not repented of results in eternal separation from God. It involves honest concern for people, a concern manifesting itself in efforts to reach them and win them to Christ and His church. In a truly evangelistic congregation there is an aura of expectancy. One Free Methodist church that lives out this concern has a back-lighted cross in its chancel. When the congregation gathers to worship on Sunday, if the cross is lighted they know that someone has been converted during the preceding week. Whenever a Free Methodist church is at its best it is permeated by this evangelistic concern.

I saw this expectancy in the Philippine church when I visited there some years ago. The Philippine annual conference on Mindanao that had appointed the Reverend Ray Streukter to begin the Manila congregation had experienced outstanding evangelistic success itself. For example, in the years 1973-1977, membership increased 140 percent. This came about because of a surge of new church plantings and visitation in new homes.

The Free Methodist Church of North America reflects concern for evangelism in its organizational structure. The Department of Evangelism and Church Growth, for example, has as its major responsibility the planting of new churches and assisting existing congregations with their outreach concerns. The denomination's 1979 General Conference gave priority to this work.

A decade later the 1989 General Conference approved a section for *The Discipline* entitled, Formation of New Churches. This statement amplifies the priority of evangelism within the Free Methodist Church which results in the formation of new congregations.

The work of evangelism cannot be done by proxy. The most vital contribution of the Department of Evangelism and Church Growth is to help local congregations to acquire the skill and will to evangelize. The reason is that evangelism is only effective when it is face to face. No one method by itself is enough. The churches that fulfil the mandate to evangelize do so with a combination of public services, house-to-house visitation, special evangelistic crusades, and caring ministries that bring the love of the church into the lives of needy people.

Evangelistic Free Methodist churches have a number of characteristics in common:

1. They are led by a pastor who is genuinely concerned that the work of evangelism be carried forward.
2. The great evangelical doctrines are believed and preached clearly, with concern for results.
3. The congregation is warm with the love of God and is united in that love.
4. The church has specific year-round programs to take the work of evangelism into its community.
5. There is provision in the church for the nurture of new Christians and their mobilization in the further work of evangelism.

We must acknowledge that 82,000 members who comprise the Free Methodist Church in North America are evangelistic as a body only when evangelistic concern and practice manifest themselves in individual congregations and conferences.

Higher Education Has a Large Place

The Methodist movement was born on a university campus. Its foremost leader, John Wesley, was a Fellow of Lincoln College, Oxford, and a scholar of eminence. It is no wonder that the Free Methodist Church, in the train of historic Methodism, has seen the importance of education and through the organization and support of institutions of higher learning has sought to fulfill its vision.

Such institutions have been a part of the Free Methodist Church from the start. Only 10 years after the organization of the church in 1860 (and long before the debate on the relationship between science and religion had come to its peak), the General Conference Committee on Education said: ". . . our usefulness must depend largely upon our knowledge of science as well as upon our knowledge of salvation. No amount of piety can atone for a want of mental culture; God never does for man what He has given him power to do for himself."

In the spirit of Methodism, the Free Methodist Church regards piety and scholarship as being compatible and in need of each other. There is no reason why Christians cannot be both tough-minded and warmhearted. The Free Methodist Church from the start has labored for the thorough Christian education of its young people.

Note, for example, that the Free Methodist Church's first general superintendent, Benjamin Titus Roberts, an honor graduate of Wesleyan University in Connecticut, was also the founder of its first school. In 1866, only six years after the Free Methodist Church began, he surrendered his home in Rochester, New York, as a down payment on a farm at North Chili, New York. This became the campus of Chili Seminary. Today, the original 30-acre site is the core of the modern 350-acre campus of Roberts Wesleyan College, ". . . a four-year liberal arts school chartered by the Regents of the University of the State of New York. It is a member of the Middle States Association of Colleges and Secondary Schools. Its Division of Nursing is accredited by the National League for Nursing and its Department of Music is a member of the National Association of Schools of Music."

As the church grew other colleges soon followed. In 1873, the village of Spring Arbor, Michigan, became the location of the second school of Free Methodism. Today, Spring Arbor College, with a spacious campus and modern buildings, is located about 10 miles west of Jackson, Michigan. It is accredited as a four-year college by the North Central Association of Colleges and Secondary Schools.

Central College is located in McPherson, Kansas. It is the oldest junior college accredited by the state of Kansas and proudly numbers among its alumni eminent people in a variety of professions and a host of dedicated Christians in many walks of life. Central College is fully accredited by the North Central Association of Colleges and Schools.

Seattle Pacific University, located in Seattle, Washington, is the largest of Free Methodism's institutions of higher learning with a student body of 3,000 plus extension programs involving several times that number. It was founded in 1891, and has a broad undergraduate program. It offers graduate training as well. Approximately one-third of the missionaries in the Free Methodist Church count Seattle Pacific University as their alma mater. Seattle Pacific is fully accredited by the Northwest Association of Secondary and Higher Schools. It is accredited by the National Council for Accreditation of Teacher Education (NCATE) at both undergraduate and graduate levels. Its nursing curriculum is accredited by both the National League for Nursing and the Washington State Board of Nursing. The School of Music is a member of the National Association of Schools of Music.

Greenville College came into being in the midwestern city of Greenville, Illinois, in 1892. It is a four-year liberal arts college with a remarkable academic record. Accredited by the North Central Association of Secondary Schools and Colleges and the National Council for Accreditation of Teacher Education, this school has received wide recognition for its academic product. A survey of 40 Christian colleges, for example, showed that more graduates of Greenville College were on their faculties than graduates of any other of the schools. Approximately 20 percent of the ministers of the Free Methodist Church have attended Greenville College.

Azusa Pacific University is affiliated with the denomination as a result of the merging of Los Angeles Pacific College, a Free Methodist school founded in 1903, with Azusa College, an institution supported by several denominations. Located in Azusa, California, it is fully accredited by the Western Association of Schools and Colleges and is recognized as an aggressive evangelical four-year institution. It has a School of Religion for the training of ministers.

Aldersgate College, overlooking Moose Jaw, Saskatchewan, was established in 1940. It is a four-year Bible College offering training for Christian ministries or church vocations through a program of biblical, general, and professional studies.

The Lorne Park College Foundation, with headquarters in Mississauga, Ontario, assists in providing grants and scholarships for students from three Canadian conferences.

John Wesley Seminary was incorporated in the State of Indiana in 1946. It functions at present as John Wesley Seminary Foundation through formal affiliations with Asbury Theological Seminary in Wilmore, Kentucky, and with Western Evangelical Seminary in Portland, Oregon. Headquarters for the foundation are at Indianapolis, but Free Methodist students are served on each campus by an assistant director of the foundation.

Approximately 100 Free Methodist ministerial students are enrolled each year in Asbury and Western and receive financial assistance through this institution.

I know firsthand that our institutions of higher learning are places of great Christian energy and purpose. Besides spending 13 years as college pastor at Greenville College, Greenville, Illinois, I've ministered on all our college campuses. I have found them committed to Christian ideals, and at the heart of each are men and women of sterling Christian character. These people are working out their Christian discipleship by serving young people in the field of Christian education.

Our schools are integrally linked to all of the other ministries of our church. This can be seen if we go back to the case of Philippine missionary Ray Streutker. Soon after his conversion in Bremerton, Washington, he spent several weeks in a ten-by-twelve-foot shack on a floating fish trap in Alaska. During that period of near solitude, he began to look into the future. What did the Lord want him to do with his life? Before he left Alaska he wrote Seattle Pacific College (now University), requesting a catalog. Thus began his pilgrimage toward a college degree, marriage to Lorraine, ordination to the Free Methodist ministry, and a life of missionary service in the Philippines.

Free Methodist People Want to Serve

Free Methodists sometimes want to serve in a larger arena than the local church, but only for a short period full-time. The church has recognized this impulse and has developed its missions programs to accommodate it. The result has been opportunities like Volunteers in Service Abroad (VISA).

At any one time there are approximately 100 short-term volunteers serving on overseas fields. These include young people who have taken a year or two away from their schooling. It includes doctors, nurses, teachers, and retired people who have a special skill to offer. These workers have been spread across the globe touching all our fields. I have seen VISA people in action in Japan sharing the load with missionaries, making special contacts with Japanese young people, and loving the Lord warmly in their service. I have met them also in Africa, the Dominican Republic, Mexico, and the Philippines, to name only a few of the fields. VISA is one of several evidences of the impulse our people have to serve.

The Free Methodist Church has also had a continuing ministry in members who go into military service. We credential active duty military chaplains and a number of reserve chaplains. These men and women are stationed with the military on land or on sea around the world, giving support to an old statement that the Free Methodist Church is the church that cares. We also have 15 institutional chaplains who serve in retirement homes, hospitals, and correctional institutions. As well as a significant group of part-time institutional chaplains.

Free Methodists Care About Social Needs

Within the expansive boundaries of Oklahoma City, Oklahoma, a modern 250-bed hospital stands six stories high on the skyline. *Deaconess Hospital* is an institution where both efficiency and warmth go into the care of the sick. I know, for I've been through the hospital, talked to patients, and heard their words of unsolicited praise.

Deaconess carries out several innovative programs. Among them are a surgical care unit set up to accommodate surgical patients on a one-day basis. There are at least 40 surgical procedures that can be done without involving an overnight stay. Savings to patients average nearly 30 percent and in some cases rise to 50 percent. (That's an angle on the Christian stewardship of money you may not have thought of.) The one-day ward has been in operation since November 1974 and has won wide recognition for its compassion and safe services.

Before leaving the unit I spoke to a woman in a bed near the exit. She was a doctor's wife in for repairs on the septum of her nose. Enthusiastically, she volunteered, "Deaconess has the best nursing care in the city." The hospital's good reputation is evidenced by the fact that it runs consistently near capacity while other hospitals in the area have many vacant beds.

Among the other innovative services carried out by Deaconess are open-heart surgery, a kidney lithotripter service, a recently added advanced obstetrical service, and nuclear medicine diagnostic procedures.

Deaconess Hospital (and the adjacent Deaconess Home for the care of unwed mothers) is not the only institution in the church where Christian love manifests itself in compassionate service. Here are some of the others.*

Heritage Village is located in the rolling hills of Western New York in the town of Gerry, near the Ohio border. It is a Christian retirement community with five levels of care. Its hospital unit alone, erected some time back at the cost of 3 million dollars, provides security and love for patients and, for its dedicated staff, an outlet for ministry.

Heritage Village Health Care Center, for example, provides both skilled nursing care and health-related nursing care for those whose physical condition requires it. The health care center is a beautiful, single-storey facility fully equipped as a modern nursing home. Accredited and licensed by the state of New York, the health care center accepts patients eligible for both Medicare and Medicaid.

Life Line Homes, Inc. with offices in Kansas City, Kansas, is an agency which provides financial assistance to churches, conferences, camps, colleges, and other agencies that are working with disadvantaged youth. Life Line attempts to meet the needs of young people in a spirit of Christian compassion and hope. It carries out its work through four specific programs: The Crisis Intervention Program, The Youth Development Program,

*See page 219 for additional agencies.

The Education Assistance Program, and The Leadership Loan Program. Life Line Homes is just one more testimony to the high value the church places on compassionate service.

Warm Beach Senior Community, set among stately cedars and other evergreens a short drive north of Seattle, provides a wide range of ministries. Residents may live independently in facilities provided or may opt for partial care; may have ward and weekly housekeeping service or, if need arises, may be admitted to the 81-bed nursing facility with round-the-clock teams of nurses and aids.

Wesley Manor in New Westminster, British Columbia, near Vancouver, and one mile from the mighty Fraser River, provides 53 single suites and nine double suites for senior citizens. It is always filled to capacity.

Woodstock Christian Care, Inc., located in Woodstock, Illinois, not far from the surging metropolis of Chicago, provides a variety of services ranging from independent living to nursing care for 170 retired people. Its day-care center approaches the day-care needs of children in our society from a Christian perspective. At the present, the licensed services care for more than 100 children whose ages range from infancy to 10 years of age. Certified teachers nurture and guide the children in a structured and secure environment.

What is the Free Methodist Church for? Among other things, it is for ministry. And these and other social agencies are extensions of the vision for ministry that is a part of every Free Methodist congregation.

A Church Rich in Camping Ministries

Campgrounds have come a long way since the days of brush arbor meetings in the nineteenth century when campers slept under a buckboard and heard enthusiastic preaching in open-air clearings. Though more sophisticated now, camps are still an important part of the work of the Free Methodist Church.

The Warm Beach Conference Grounds of the Pacific Northwest Conference, for example, covering 200 acres, is the outstanding Christian center of the northwestern United States. Its excellent facilities accommodate two family camps each summer, with an attendance totalling 1,500. There are 18 weeks of camps for boys and girls--as well as youth camps, seven adult camps for senior citizens, and weekend retreat ministries. The expansive camp lodge, center of the program, is in use 11 months of the year.

Throughout North America, there are 56 Free Methodist campgrounds for family camp activities. In addition, the conferences hold at least 40 youth camps, 45 camps for young teens, and 55 camps for Christian Life Club (CLC) cadets. Most of these are specialized events, separate from family camp.

Remarkable things happen on Free Methodist campgrounds. Away from the haste and noise of modern life, young people hear God's call to ministry, families are reconciled, and backsliders are reclaimed to God. Lifelong friendships often begin in God's great outdoors. Young adults sometimes meet marriage partners.

Camps vary from area to area. They take on the character of the conferences they serve and can be found in all stages of development. But all Free Methodist camps are dedicated to thoroughly Christian ends. Camps are an integral part of the church's ministry.

A Ministering Church Needs a Ministries Center

Every serious enterprise needs a center. It's just a fact of life. Whether it's a school district, modern farm, or multinational business, if all phases of the enterprise are to work toward a common end, they must have a center where vision is generated, plans are coordinated, and energies given direction.

The Free Methodist Church has its World Ministries Center near interstates 65, 69, 70, 74, and 465 on the west side of Indianapolis, Indiana. At 770 N. High School Road, it's only seven minutes from an international airport. This neat and modest-appearing building houses a diligent company of Christ's disciples. Each of them works to facilitate the world-encircling ministries of the Free Methodist Church.

For example, toward the back of the building on the first floor is the World Missions Department. Here, under the guidance of a director, the needs of missionaries in many countries are attended to. There are inquiries to be answered, long-distance phone calls to be made, "missionary kids" to be contacted here stateside, budgets to be serviced. The tasks are numerous and complex. For example, the department may learn that here at home the aged parent of a veteran missionary has died. The missionary is serving on the other side of the globe. Contacts must be made immediately and plane tickets ordered. Or a new mission field has opened quite spontaneously in Cameroon or Bolivia or any one of a score of other places. The calls for help come to this department. Or a military coup in some particular country signals that all our missionaries must be brought out immediately. You can't just leave these problems to care for themselves. Someone must be ready to act. That's the sort of work a World Missions Department oversees.

Similar things can be said for the Department of Christian Education. If kindergarten children in Maine or Idaho are to be taught the ways of Christ, this will call for uniform curricula. And, if we are to make sex education available in our churches or provide information on the problems of drug abuse, there must be a center where these needs are addressed.

Consider the issue of spreading the gospel by planting new churches. Between 1985 and 1990, 236 churches were planted. But the goal must be promoted and church planters must be provided with useful resources. That's another reason for a World Ministries Center.

The World Ministries Center is located in Indianapolis, a thriving midwestern city. Our whole world is becoming increasingly urban and location affects outlook. When the World Missions Department communicates with missionaries in Brazil, they contact Sao Paulo, a city whose metropolitan population exceeds 15 million people. And when the Christian Education Department prepares a curriculum for high school students, it knows that growing numbers of them will be in North America's troubled cities. The work going on in the World Ministries Center doesn't overlook the needs of rural or suburban America. Nor does it diminish them. But it knows that today cities must be carefully targeted.

How You May Be
More Deeply a Part of the Extended Family

Specialists on the family warn us repeatedly of the limitations of the nuclear family--mother, father, and a child or two. Children, they say, need a bigger community to aid their development. They need an extended family--parents plus grandparents, uncles, aunts, cousins, and close family friends.

The same may be true for developing Christians. They need their own local church to support them and give them opportunities for ministry. But when the universal church of Christ now has stations in every country of the world, growing Christians can't afford to narrow down their interest exclusively to one congregation. They need a larger context for their prayers and concerns.

This is what the Free Methodist Church offers to you--a larger context for your prayers and concerns. It can be an extended family of 82,000 brothers and sisters in North America and a quarter of a million if overseas churches are included. You will never meet all of them, but you are linked with them in a ministry bigger than any one congregation can achieve.

Here are suggestions to help you to become more involved with your extended family.

1. *Read.*

Light and Life Press carries out a major service to the denomination in making literature available to the churches on a regular basis. This material is printed to instruct, inform, enrich, and by doing so to supplement all the efforts expended at the local level for the building up of the church.

As a new Christian, whatever your pre-Christian habits may have been, you should plan to include some good reading in your daily fare. Good reading nourishes the mind and spirit like roast beef nourishes the body. In that new reading program, you will want to include material that acquaints you with your church.

The *Light and Life Magazine* should be high on your list. It carries first-person accounts, often written by other Free Methodists. And it carries meatier articles for the exercise of your mental faculties and the enlargement of your understanding. In each issue you'll find a short piece by one of your bishops, and inside the back cover, an editorial. News of the churches, accomplishments of other Free Methodists, schedules, letters-- there is helpful information in every issue.

Light and Life is not your only source of knowledge about the church. The *Missionary Tidings* will keep you posted on the missionary enterprise of the denomination. Take note of items of interest in the *Free Methodist Ministries Update*. In Canada, the *Free Methodist Herald* gives a national slant on the church.

You may not keep up with all these papers. But you will gain valuable information and inspiration by reading something from them regularly.

2. *Make your skills available.*

In every conference there are programs that need workers. A CLC camp for children, for example, must have a large staff of teachers, counsellors, athletic directors, chaplains, cooks, and more. You may have a skill that could be greatly used in this sort of ministry. If you make it available you will become acquainted, in the process, with Christians from other Free Methodist churches.

Of course, "charity begins at home," and your first duty will always be to your home church. Christians who are ready to pour out their energies for a distant cause while being only shadowy presences in their home church are like parents who show compassion to their neighbor's children while their own go shoeless. But there is no need to do only one or the other. You may be able to share your skills in your own congregation and offer a ministry to the conference or denomination as well.

3. *Attend a larger church gathering occasionally.*

Periodically, Free Methodist young people from all across North America converge on a city--Toronto, Saint Louis, or elsewhere--for a Holiday Teen Convention. Frequently a denominational youth camp is held and hundreds fly or drive in. The General Missionary Board sponsors regional celebrations. Conferences sponsor family camps. General Conference is held every four years. Though you couldn't possibly attend all of them, gatherings like these need to have a place in your schedule. They will help you to see your church in a larger perspective. And you'll be inspired.

4. *Participate in the mission and ministries of the church.*

You may already have the habit of paying a tithe of your income to the Lord's work and presenting it to Him through the budget of your home church. Every time you place an offering in the offering plate, a portion of your gift goes to support the larger mission of the Free Methodist Church.

If you saw a list of all the ministries you support in this manner, you would be surprised. A portion of your offering goes toward scholarships for ministerial students in seminary, another portion to the pension program for retired ministers. A portion may help to buy a Land Rover for a Central African mission, and another portion may go toward the salary of the general director of Christian Education Department here in North America. By pooling resources in this way, North America's 82,000 Free Methodists carry on a great list of ministries.

Make offering time a special prayer time every Sunday. This will increase your sense of involvement in the worldwide work of your church.

5. *Pray.*

A denomination can too easily become little more than a sociological group. If its membership has a core of second-generation and third-generation people and these are linked by common ideas and values, the task is almost accomplished. Good communications, imaginative programs, and strong promotion will finish it.

But it takes more than these emphases, valuable as they are, to make a denomination a spiritual force in the world.

The message of the Scriptures must be preached and taught with power and received in faith: God loves all mankind and wills that all should be saved. But He does not accomplish this purpose by himself. He has a servant people in the world and they are entrusted with the stewardship of His gospel--until the end of the age. If the Free Methodist Church is to be a spiritual force, it must be regularly renewed in faith and mission.

And that is where you come in. You can pray daily for your church locally and around the world. Pray for your pastor and all other leaders in your home church. Pray for other churches in your conference and the superintendent who guides them. Intercede for the ministries outlined in this chapter. The Apostle Paul wrote to the Colossian Christians, "We have heard of your faith in Christ Jesus and of the love you have for all the saints" (Colossians 1:4). There's the picture of big-hearted Christians. Be like them in your prayers.

Pray especially for church planters in your conference, youth workers who give their energies to minister to needy young people and missionaries your church is supporting. This is the deepest way to express the fact that you belong.

For Review:

1. There are how many Free Methodists, how many congregations, and how many conferences in North America?

2. Indicate the name and location of the seven North American institutions of higher learning which are part of the Free Methodist Church.

3. Identify the following: VISA, Deaconness Home, Heritage Village, Life Line Homes, and Wesley Manor.

4. Where is the location of the denomination's headquarters and publishing house?

5. Name several denominational periodicals.

6. What are five things you can do to become more involved in your church as extended family?

7. Our denomination has how many missionaries on how many fields?

For Further Reading:

Refer to the current *Yearbook* of the Free Methodist Church for comprehensive statistics regarding denominational programs and activities.

My Church Brochure Series: *Social Concerns* and *To Care, To Love, To Share*. Indianapolis, Indiana: Light and Life Press.

For Further Thought:

Rapidly review this chapter, close your eyes, and think of as many ministries as possible of your extended family throughout North America and the world.

Additional Agencies:

Clawson Manor, New Life, Inc., is an apartment building for well elderly senior citizens at Clawson, Michigan, with *179* efficiency units and *85* bedroom units.

Olive Branch Mission, in Chicago, Illinois, is the nation's oldest rescue mission, dedicated to aiding the destitute and rescuing the fallen and outcasts. It maintains Christian evangelistic worship services, besides the giving out of clothing and food for the needy.

Glossary of Theological Terms

AUTHORITY OF THE BIBLE--the conviction that the Bible is the sufficient and final resource for what we should believe and how we should live. It is the final word regarding such matters as God, man, sin, salvation, the Christian life, and the future.

DISPENSATIONALISM--an elaborate system of interpretation and theology of recent orgin, which divides the Scriptures into seven dispensations in which eight different covenants between God and man are claimed to operate. The system is imposed on the Scriptures rather than growing naturally out of the Scriptures. It ignores the usual division of Scriptures into two covenants (Old and New Testaments). It also spawns a theory of the future centered on Israel as a nation rather than on the Church and the World. Prophecy is interpreted to fit the dispensational scheme.

ENTIRE SANCTIFICATION (see sanctification also)--the work of the Holy Spirit by which the fully consecrated believer, through the faith in Christ, is cleansed of inward sin, enabling him to love God wholly and his neighbor as himself. Christian growth leads to the moment of cleansing, and entire sanctification perpares one for greater spiritual growth. It is a crisis point in the ongoing process of sanctification.

IMMANENT (see transcendent also)--the infinite God dwells *within* (immanent) as well as *above* the universe (transcendent). Keeping these two concepts together saves us from pantheism which equates God and the universe, and from deism which says God created the universe but has gone off and left it to itself.

IMPART--that we are made righteous by an act of God actually changing us and providing the constant grace for a new life in Christ. It infers that we cannot be righteous by our own doing and that imputed righteousness alone is not enough.

IMPUTE--a legal illustrative word suggesting the transfer of real value from the account of one person to that of another. Though the sinner is bankrupt of righteousness, the righteousness of Christ is credited to his account. Some theological perspectives lay major emphases on imputed righteousness. This tends to make righteousness artificial rather than real.

INCARNATE--God enfleshed; the union of God and man in visible human form in the person of Jesus Christ.

REPROBATION--a state of rejection. One is considered unfit, unable to do good, and therefore, disqualified from relationship with God and condemned to eternal punishment.

SANCTIFICATION (see entire sanctifaction also)--is what the Spirit of Christ (Holy Spirit) does to make us holy and like himself in love. It includes both cleansing and being set apart unto God. Sanctification begins at conversion and continues throughtout the Christian's life.

TRANSCENDENT (see immanent also)--that which surpasses or goes beyond all other things. God is not a man nor a part of the created universe. He is greater than man and the universe. His power surpasses any demand that can be placed upon it. He is beyond human understanding. God must assist us in even the limited understanding we have of Him.